S0-BJA-049

the future starts now

The Renewable Organization™ for Faith-Based Groups

A Renewal Enterprise, Inc.

books

Other books in The Renewable Organization™ Series:

- *Seeing Through New Eyes: Using PAWN Process™ in Faith-Based Groups*
- *Do What Matters: The 4-D Cycle™ for Faith-Based Groups*

The Renewable Practices™ Series for Faith-Based Groups

- *19 (or more) Ideas for Asking Purposeful Questions*
- *19 (or more) Ideas for Using Participative Processes*
- *19 (or more) Ideas for Working Playfully*
- *19 (or more) Ideas for Taking Place Seriously*
- *19 (or more) Ideas for Being Reproductive*
- *19 (or more) Ideas for Seeing Possibilities*
- *19 (or more) Ideas for Igniting Passion*

Other books by the authors of *The Future Starts Now: The Renewable Organization™ for Faith-Based Groups:*

Fryer, K. **Dancing Down the Hallway: Spiritual Reflections for the Everyday**. Augsburg Fortress, 2001.

Fryer, K. **Reclaiming the "L" Word: Renewing the Church from its Lutheran Core.** Augsburg Fortress, 2003.

Fryer, K., Dave Daubert. **A Story Worth Sharing: Engaging Evangelism.** Minneapolis: Augsburg Fortress, 2004.

Fryer, K. **No Experience Necessary: 8 Unit Bible Study.** Minneapolis: Augsburg Fortress, 2005.

Fryer, K. **Reclaiming the "C" Word: Daring to Be Church Again.** Minneapolis: Augsburg Fortress, 2006.

Daubert, D. **Living Lutheran: Renewing Your Congregation.** Minneapolis: Augsburg Fortress, 2007.

Fryer, K. **No Experience Necessary. Everybody's Welcome.** Revised and expanded. Minneapolis: Augsburg Fortress, 2007.

Fryer, K. **Reclaiming the "E" Word: Waking Up to Our Evangelical Identity.** Minneapolis: Augsburg Fortress, 2008.

Daubert, D., Tana Kjos. **Reclaiming the "V" Word: Renewing Life At Its Vocational Core** Minneapolis: Augsburg Fortress, 2009.

Visit the A.R.E. blog at www.arenewalenterprise.com for a ton of free articles and also to learn more about how you can put the principles, practices and processes of a Renewable Organization™ to work in your faith community, congregation, judicatory, denomination, faith-based school or agency.

the
future
starts
now

The Renewable Organization™
for Faith-Based Groups

Contributors:

Dave Daubert

Marlene Daubert

Kelly A. Fryer

Tana Kjos

Robert Machamer

Catherine Pate

Jennifer Lee Robinson

Production Editor:

Catherine Pate

Layout and Design:

Instant Noodles Design

Scribe:

Kelly A. Fryer

Published by A Renewal Enterprise, Inc.

A Renewal Enterprise, Inc.,
40 E. 9th Street #1416,
Chicago, Illinois 60605, U.S.A.

First published in 2009 by A Renewal Enterprise, Inc.

Copyright© A Renewal Enterprise, Inc., 2009
All rights reserved.

Unless otherwise noted, scripture quotations are from *New Revised Standard Version* Bible, copyright ©1989 National Council of the Churches of Christ in the United States of America. Used by permission. All rights reserved. The use of italics with scripture references denotes a paraphrase rather than direct quotation.

Without limiting the rights under copyright reserved above, no part of this publication may be reproduced, stored in or introduced into a retrieval system, or transmitted, in any form or by any means (electronic, mechanical, photocopying, recording, or otherwise), without the prior written permission of the copyright owner and publisher of this book.

The scanning, uploading and distribution of this book via the Internet or via any other means without the permission of the publisher is illegal and punishable by law. Please purchase only authorized electronic editions and do not participate in or encourage electronic piracy of copyrightable materials. Your support of the authors' rights is appreciated.

Produced and printed in Canada. ISBN: 978-0-9842356-0-5

For every person who ever said,
"I think I can."

Contents

11   Introduction

19   Chapter 1   **The Future Starts Now**

31   Chapter 2   **An Invitation to Freedom**

43   Chapter 3   **Making the Shift**

59   Chapter 4   **A New Way of Being**

77   Chapter 5   **A New Way of Seeing**

97   Chapter 6   **A New Way of Doing**

117   Afterword: **Stranger Things Have Happened**

123   Reading List/Bibliography

125   Acknowledgements

127   Who Are We?

Introduction

The world around us is changing at lightning speed. No one can keep up. In recent times, we have even seen institutions everybody thought were "too big to fail" topple over. What is the future of the institutional church—including your congregation, judicatory or faith-based group—in the midst of this changing context? No one knows.

This is an era of seismic cultural change, and there isn't a single aspect of life today that isn't changing with it. Remember that bookshelf of encyclopedias you (or your grandparents) had when you were a kid?—Gone. It's been replaced by an online encyclopedia created by the collaborative effort of people like you (and your smartest friends), which researchers agree is on its way to becoming as reliable as the best print version you can buy. Wikipedia is doing more than saving trees and clearing bookshelves, though. It's changing the way people think about authority, organization, information and community. It's making us believe that our ideas and our input mean something. But that's just one example of how everything around us is changing.

Mom and pop travel agencies started disappearing almost overnight once the internet gave individuals the ability to access the same information they previously needed an expert to provide them. Most independently owned bookstores have floated down the proverbial Amazon. Bottom-up digital health care systems (sometimes called *Heath 2.0*) that allow people to rate their doctors[1] and give people unprecedented access to medical information are empowering and equipping people to self-diagnose and self-treat; challenging the opinions of leaders and the medical establishment; transforming the paternalistic relationship doctors have traditionally had with their patients and reforming the field of medicine in ways that some authorities argue are both "profound and unstoppable."[2]

Education and technology leaders (called *edupunks* by some observers) are threatening to make the on-campus university obsolete as they experiment with "open education" and "peer-to-peer learning." They are seeking ways to give everyone access to higher education regardless of geography or social and economic status, by delivering it cheaper, faster and online.[3]

Environmental concerns are changing the way everything from transportation to sanitation is done.

There is virtually no area of life, work or play anywhere in the world that is not in the midst of being transformed by technology and connectivity, globalization, and the realization that people can't keep treating the planet, or each other, like they're disposable.

Thomas Friedman, author of *The World is Flat: A Brief History of the 21st Century*, says one day people will look back on this time as "one of those fundamental shifts or inflection points, like Gutenberg's invention of the printing press, the rise of the nation-state, or the Industrial Revolution—each of which, in its day, produced changes in the role of individuals, the forms and functions of governments, religions and the arts, the ways in which business was conducted and wars were fought, the role of women, and the way science and research were conducted…"[4]

All around us today, we see businesses scrambling to figure out what these changes mean for them. Schools, hospitals, non-profit organizations and government agencies are doing their best to keep up. The most entrepreneurial souls are hoping to be on the front end of whatever the next curve is in order to capitalize on the opportunities they see there.

What would make somebody think the church is immune from all this? Why would you want to be?

If you picked up this book because you think we can bail out your church or the faith-based organization you care about, you're going to be deeply disappointed. Besides, what the church needs today isn't a bailout. It needs a backbone. The church needs to be brave enough to ask the right questions, to listen for what God is saying, and to step into this emerging future, confident in God's promise and power. The church needs to stop fighting over things that don't matter and clinging to structures that don't work anymore. The church needs to be ready to follow wherever God leads next.

We have some ideas that we think can help.

This book has been written to introduce you—our friends, colleagues, clients and co-workers in faith communities and faith-based groups across Canada and the U.S.—to the theological propositions, principles, practices and processes of what we call The Renewable Organization. At the heart of this system are three principles for helping you and the organization you care about:

- **Be who you are;**
- **See what you have;**
- **Do what matters.**

This is our contribution to helping organizations of all types and sizes, including churches, treat people and the planet we share with respect and dignity.

The Renewable Organization system helps nurture organizations, movements and communities that are as genuinely human as the people in them. It teaches leaders to set people free to use their gifts in ways that make a real difference in the organizations they care about and in the world. It helps leaders learn how to tap into and unleash the energy that dwells within the people they encounter for the sake of doing what really matters.

We believe it can prepare you to move confidently, collaboratively and creatively into God's emerging future.

This system, like the worldview that characterizes everything we think, say and do, has emerged and is emerging as we are encountered by the living Word. For most of our lives, each one of us on the ARE team has been wrestling with, listening to, learning from and transformed by the God who meets us in scripture.

The biblical stories are *our* stories, as much as any tale told at a family reunion. They describe, decipher and give voice to what is true about *us*. They are the lens through which we see and understand everything.

We have also built this system on the basis of what we have learned and observed in our (100+!) combined years of experience leading and working with churches and other organizations. It has been shaped (and is constantly being reshaped) by the rich and growing diversity of educational and professional experience of our team members, who have been trained and/or worked in the fields of congregational leadership, design, engineering, economics, social work, the arts, psychology, business, political science, education and theology/missiology.

As we have developed this system and the ideas behind it, we have been listening in on

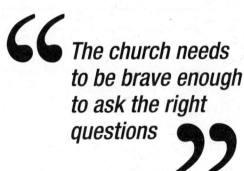

The church needs to be brave enough to ask the right questions

the conversations happening in both the missional and emerging church movements; some of us have taught, written and wrestled with those who at one time or another have been members of the Gospel and Our Culture Network.[5] We have been especially influenced by their clear articulation of the nature and mission of God, who "seeks to be in relational community with all people in his [sic] creation,"[6] picking up where the great 20th century missionary and missiologist Lesslie Newbigin left off; and by their insistence that God's mission is the proper framework within which to understand the purpose of the church. But our paths diverge after this point in significant ways, both theologically and theoretically.

Following the work of Newbigin's foil, another great 20th century missionary and missiologist named JC Hoekendijk, our theology is much more "worldly." For us, the world is not the *object* of God's mission or of the church's activity. The world is not a problem to be solved. And our job isn't to "do" something to or "take" something to "fix" the world. We believe the world is where the action is and that our job, as the church, is mostly to have eyes to see and courage to name what God is up to so that we and others can participate in what God is already doing.[7]

Largely because of this theological shift, we have also grown increasingly distant from the modern approach to organization theory that has influenced and, in some cases, defined the approach that has been used by missiologists engaged in congregational and judicatory consulting over the past several decades.[8] This consumable approach, at its core, objectifies the world, treating the environment like it's a threat to your organization. Since resources are thought to be scarce, your challenge is basically to figure out how to get your share (before the church down the street does) in order to survive. You do that by being more relevant and providing better services to meet the needs of people in your context. Even though many years ago we started out using this approach, we simply no longer can support or encourage the kind of thinking that we believe both characterizes and produces a consumable approach to life and work.

Instead we have become very excited about the emergent and organic approaches that are bubbling up in a variety of fields. We have discovered a special and deep affinity for the research being done today in the field of social innovation (which inspires and educates leaders to champion and work for transformative social change, especially that which re-engages vulnerable populations) at places like Social Innovation Generation at the University of

Waterloo, Ontario, and the Center for Social Innovation at Stanford University; by symbolic-interpretive and postmodern organization theorists like Mary Jo Hatch and Margaret Wheatley and by contemporary management experts like MIT's Thomas Malone, all of whom are making strong research-based arguments for decentralization in the workplace, as both the preferred and the inevitable future. These voices, for the most part, have not been part of the missional conversation happening in the church today; this is a great loss and something we hope to change. You will see their fingerprints throughout this book.

We cannot emphasize enough what a radical shift in both theology and in theory this has been and continues to be—for us and for the church leaders we are working with. Even though our approach is post-missional (in the way that it builds on but moves beyond the Newbigin-inspired theology of the late 20th century) and postmodern (in the way it diverges from the predominant approach to organization theory), people often just don't 'get it.' Sometimes, as we're describing to someone the practices or processes we're using, he or she will interrupt us and say something like, "Oh yeah! I see what you're saying! That's just like when I was serving at

_____(the last place they served/worked)!" Then he or she will tell us the story and, sure enough, we can see traces of the consumable theological and theoretical ideas that we believe have gotten the church into its current mess and will prevent us from entering the emerging future. The world, in their story, was a problem to be solved—and their church worked together to solve it. The leap to a new way of seeing the world as the arena of God's activity and thinking about their role in it as a co-creator in God's mission with God and with the world was just too far.

We are working hard to make this leap possible. In this book, we've tried to make very complex theological and theoretical ideas both accessible and practical so that they can have real-life and real-world impact. We are available to: teach this system, coach and consult with you and your leaders, and design and facilitate processes that can help you make this shift no matter what type or size your organization happens to be.

You don't have to be a Christian, a person of any particular faith or of any faith at all to use this system. As you read this book or use other Renewable Organization resources you may find yourself wanting to use them in another non-profit organization or business you care about.

But we do have a special passion for sharing what we know and what we do with leaders in progressive and mainstream churches and faith-based organizations. Although we come from diverse backgrounds, every single one of us has a decade or more of hands-on experience working, leading, teaching and/or volunteering in faith-based organizations, including theological seminaries, local congregations, judicatory and denominational offices, social service agencies and parachurch organizations. We understand the challenges facing faith-based organizations, especially those in the mainstream of religious culture in North America today.

Each of us who has contributed to this book is located by tradition and by choice within the stream of Christianity that, at its best, over the centuries has preached and practiced a message of scandalous love, radical freedom and profound responsibility to neighbour. Our lives and our work are shaped by these five theological propositions:

• **This is God's gig**—Throughout the Hebrew Scriptures and the New Testament, we meet a God who has a dream for us and for all creation. Jesus came to announce and to accomplish a new "kingdom" in which the last will be first, the hungry will be filled, the outcast will be welcomed with open arms and death will not have the final word. This is God's agenda. It is the only agenda that matters.

• **God is on the loose**—God will not conform to our expectations or be confined by our walls, our wishes or our rituals. Acts 2 was not an anomaly. The whole biblical story tells us that God is at work in and through all kinds of people and places, even when we are unaware of it. That is also the experience of our lives. The world is not a place to be avoided or conquered. It is the arena of God's activity. We meet God "out there," no less than we meet God "in here," within the community of faith. And so we engage the world with eyes wide open, on the lookout for what God is up to in the midst of the everyday.

• **Our lives matter**—The biblical story tells us that God never works alone. One of the very first things Jesus did was to gather together a group of women and men to work alongside him. We are called to participate in what God is up to in the world, as a community of faith and in our everyday lives, to name it when we see it and to jump in to help in any way we can. This call is a gift because it comes to each of us freely without precondition. And this gift is a call because it defines our purpose and gives our lives and our work meaning.

• **Jesus sets us free**—In and through Jesus, we have been set free from sin, death, fear and anything else that separates us from God and from each other.

There is no Jew or Gentile, black or white, male or female, rich or poor, gay or straight, old or young. We are all children of the same heavenly parent. We are called to live like this is true and to share this good news with everyone.

• **We could be wrong**—The God who comes to meet us in Jesus was nailed to a tree but will not be nailed down by our pious proclamations. In fact, the cross teaches us that this God turns upside down our every idea about who God is and what God is supposed to look like and how God is supposed to act. As soon as we are convinced that we have all the answers, we are as wrong as we could possibly be. And so we engage our work and our world with a kind of bold humility, confident enough to say what we believe, smart enough to know we might be wrong, and eager to learn from those who see things differently than we do.

You will see glimpses of these propositions at work, shaping the principles and practices presented throughout this book.

The book itself is divided into six chapters. In Chapter 1, we'll talk about the importance of recognizing the treasure of extraordinary power in these clay jars (i.e., our faith-based organizations and communities, and our own lives). Chapter 2 builds a theological framework for The Renewable Organization using the story of Jesus' call to the disciples in Matthew 4 as an illustration of what that looks like. Chapter 3 describes the shift from a consumable approach to life, work and ministry to a renewable one. Chapter 4 introduces seven practices that you can use within your organization to unleash the power that dwells within you (i.e., be who you are). In Chapter 5 we'll share a process that will help you learn to discern God's direction for you in any context (i.e., see what you have). And in Chapter 6 we'll teach you a process strategy for moving from discernment to action (i.e., do what matters). At the end of each chapter are reflection questions that use the three lenses described in Chapter 5 (God, your neighbour, and yourself) to help you wrestle with what you're learning and begin to see things in a new way.

At A Renewal Enterprise we are learning together what it means to be who we are and see what we have for the sake of doing what matters…in our own lives, in the organizations we care about and in the world we all share.

We are excited about being on this journey with you. We are praying for you as you bring your faith community along for the adventure. We don't pretend to have all the answers for how to get where we're going. Nobody does. But we have reason to believe that the theological propositions, principles, practices and processes of The Renewable Organization are a good place to start.

The Back Story

[1] National Public Radio, "New Web Site Lets Patients Rate Their Doctors," August 14, 2009.

[2] In an issue of the *British Medical Journal* which was devoted largely to this topic …, Joanne Shaw, a prominent figure in the British medical establishment, argues that "traditional paternalistic relationships between patients and doctors are being undermined in much the same way as the religious Reformation of the 16th century empowered the laity and threatened the 1,000-year-old hierarchy of the Catholic church in Europe. The Reformation had irreversible consequences for Western society; the implications of the health-care reformation could also be profound." Fiona Godlee, the journal's editor, agrees that the shift towards patient empowerment is "unstoppable." From "Health 2.0," *The Economist*, April 16, 2009.

[3] Anya Kamenetz, "How Web-Savvy Edupunks Are Transforming American Higher Education," Fast Company, (September 2009): p. 138.

[4] Thomas L. Friedman, *The World is Flat: A Brief History of the Twentieth Century.* (New York: Picador. 2007), p. 49.

[5] The Gospel and Our Culture Network exists to "provide useful research regarding the encounter between the gospel and our culture, and to encourage local action" (from the website www.gocn.org). Although this ecumenical network of scholars and practitioners has become far more diffuse than it was in the 1990s, and its members are moving in different directions, both theologically and theoretically, its influence in the work and lives of those who were a part of it—and/or have learned and worked with those who were—has been significant.

[6] Craig Van Gelder, *The Ministry of the Missional Church: A Community Led by the Spirit,* (Baker Books, Grand Rapids, MI, 2007), p. 110.

[7] How you understand the relationship between church and context is profoundly important. It shapes the way you understand the nature and purpose of the church; church leadership and organization; how you approach change, planning and evangelism; and every single aspect of how you live and work together.

What has been missing (or at least anemic) in the dominant missiological conversation of the past several decades, from our perspective, is the reality that God is on the loose in the world. Consequently, the world is viewed as the object of God's mission and of the church's activity, rather than the arena in which God is actually at work.

[cf. Van Gelder describes six theological points which sum up this prevailing perspective: 1) The nature of the Triune God is relational, 2) God seeks to be in relationship with all creation, 3) God sent Jesus Christ "into the world to defeat the power of sin and bring about the possibility of reconciliation of all persons and the redemption of every dimension of life within creation," and "the church is to participate in this redemptive work of God" through "a ministry of suffering service and cruciform discipleship," 4) Christ is at the center of "this reconciling and redemptive work of God" which is "present in the kingdom of God" 5) The Spirit is at work in the world right now "in relationship to a gathered community, the church," which is a "sign," a "foretaste" and an "instrument" of the kingdom, and 6) The "redemptive reign" of God "will some day come to consummation in God's time." It is "now" and "not yet." (pp. 110-111).]

[8] Van Gelder, for example, favours "an open systems perspective, an approach which studies the relationship between an organization and its environment. Within this framework, resource dependency theory is helpful to congregations for understanding their relationship to their context, where a congregation has to secure sufficient resources from its environment in order to maintain viability," (Van Gelder, p. 113, referencing Mary Jo Hatch, *Organization Theory*, pp. 63-100.) This theory, in other words, views the relationship between organization and environment as being inherently adversarial—and resources are viewed through the lens of scarcity.

At its very worst, here's how the resource dependency theory works: Your church has to acquire resources or "inputs" (e.g., people, dollars, etc.) from the environment in order to produce more goods and services or "outputs" than the church down the street so that you can acquire enough resources or "inputs" (e.g., people, dollars, etc.) from the environment in order to survive. If you are not relevant or effective enough—if you don't produce good enough "outputs"—that church down the street will. And they will get the resources instead of you. And you will die. Now, Van Gelder does warn that this theory—and others from within the social sciences—must be "critiqued for its usefulness in light of the biblical-theological framework." (p. 113) However, from our perspective, the biblical-theological framework that dominates the missiological conversation today (see above) actually tends to support the resource dependency theory and edits it mainly inasmuch as the Holy Spirit becomes an additional "input" that enables the local congregation to "output" goods and services that are useful in God's mission. Some missiologists (for example, Alan Roxburgh, a pastor/teacher/writer from British Columbia, and his team at the Allelon Missional Leadership Network; and Patrick Keifert from Church Innovations) have started leaning towards a more organic, postmodern approach to organization theory. Keifert warns against "the objectification of persons and communities," for example (*We Are Here Now: A New Missional Era,* Allelon Publishing, Eagle, Idaho, 2006). Roxburgh argues that current (i.e. modernist) approaches to leadership and organizations are "inadequate to forming a missional church" and wants to see leadership that "cultivates an environment that innovates and releases the missional imagination present among a community of God's people"—a decidedly post-modernist approach to leadership (*The Missional Leader: Equipping Your Church to Reach a Changing World,* Jossey-Bass, San Francisco, 2006, p. 5). But shaking off the dominant modernist approach is difficult, even with the best of intentions, when your theological perspective has an exaggerated view of the role of the church in God's mission, coupled with an anemic view of the world as the arena of God's activity. So far, we have not yet heard anyone in the missiological conversation articulate a truly organic and emergent approach to being and doing church. We will let the reader determine whether or not we are successful, but that is our intention in this book. .

The Future Starts Now

"But we have this treasure in clay jars, so that it may be made clear that this extraordinary power belongs to God and does not come from us." — 2 Cor. 4:7

There is a pastor on the northwest side of Chicago who has taken an extraordinary and difficult route to ordination because of his denomination's policies regarding sexual orientation. Even though that denomination has recently changed its policies, he knows there are still a lot of congregations that won't accept him. He is, in the eyes of many church folk, an imperfect and even undesirable candidate for ministry.

The congregation he's serving doesn't care what anybody else thinks about him. That could be because they're used to being told that they are an imperfect and undesirable congregation.

Several years ago, at the time he was applying to be their pastor, their membership had dribbled down to about a dozen people, and their budget had become so unbalanced that, when graphed, it made the Leaning Tower of Pisa look steady. This unlikely pastor and his unattractive congregation seemed made for each other. And hardly anyone expected anything good to come of the match.

But this young pastor knew better. He really believed that God was calling him into ordained ministry. He trusted God to do amazing, surprising and wonderful things in and through him wherever he was called to serve. "And if God can do this through me," he challenged his new congregation, "he can do this through you, too."

Together, this pastor and the people of that congregation are taking some holy risks. They are learning how to ask purposeful questions. They are prayerfully trying to discern God's direction. They are daring to follow wherever they sense God leading.

These days, they are making music and art with kids in their community, they are connecting with families in their neighbourhood, and they are on the front lines in the fight for social service spending in their city.

Although today, this little congregation has more than a dozen members and their numbers keep growing, it isn't clear to us what their future will be. They may or may not be the next Chicago area megachurch—that may or may not be *God's* vision for them (and if it isn't, who cares?!).

But together they are learning some very important things: They are discovering how to *be who they are and see what they have for the sake of doing what matters.* They are doing whatever they can with what they've got to be useful to God. They have come to believe (at least on their good days) that, no matter what anybody else thinks or says, there is an extraordinary power at work within them. And they seem committed to putting that power to good use no matter what tomorrow holds.

Unleash the power within you

This book is built on a couple of assumptions. One of them is that God is real and on the loose in this world, reconciling the whole creation and setting people free. A second is that God calls and empowers each one of us to participate in that mission.

This is the story we read in the Hebrew Scriptures, beginning with God's call to that frisky first couple to tend the earth and care for one another. It is the testimony we hear echoing across the ages through the voices of giants like Martin Luther and John Wesley, Hans Hauge and Soren Kierkegaard, Dietrich Bonhoeffer, Lesslie Newbigin and J.C. Hoekendijk, Dorothy Day, Martin Luther King, Jr. and the remarkable women of Selma, Alabama—maids and nannies and labourers—who stubbornly refused to let their frightened pastors cave under the pressure to get back on those buses and let the segregationists win. All of them, in one way or another, put everything they had on the line, believing that God is up to something in this world, something good and holy and true, and that they were being called to participate in it somehow.

This is the story that has been passed down to us by our grandparents, teachers and friends. It has been the experience of our own lives. It is the assumption Paul was making, too, when he wrote to those clay jars in Corinth.

The Christian community in Corinth was a mess. It seemed to be constantly in crisis. Divided into factions, it was being torn apart by differences over theology, piety, personality and basic human foolishness. "It has been reported to me by

Chloe's people," Paul scolded, "that there are quarrels among you, my brothers and sisters. What I mean is that each of you says, 'I belong to Paul,' or 'I belong to Apollos,' or 'I belong to Cephas,' or 'I belong to Christ.'" (1 Corinthians 1:11-12)

Each little faction insisted its members were the best, the brightest and the most spiritually mature. They tore each other down. They were petty and jealous of one another. They made up stupid things to fight about. (Sound like any churches you know?) In fact, their arguments and their behaviours were so ridiculous that Paul couldn't resist: *You're acting like a bunch of bratty children.* And he was right, they were. The ironic thing is that Paul wasn't even referring to the Corinthians as "clay jars." He was talking about himself.

> ## What is God's purpose for us?

Paul was a smart guy—a lawyer. But he wasn't always good with people. He could be arrogant, and he had a stubborn streak that got him into trouble even with his closest friends. The message he had to proclaim was radical, to be sure. But the way he proclaimed his message was, well, sometimes just as problematic. And so Paul, the guy a lot of people were counting on (not to mention funding) to get the word out about Jesus, kept getting himself into hot water; thrown out of town, hauled off to prison, beaten up by angry crowds.

His financial backers, especially the church leaders in Philippi, wondered if they were betting on the wrong horse. He had to send one of his co-workers to assure them that he was getting the job done, in spite of what looked like one disaster after another (Phil. 1:12-14, 2:25). And a lot of other people, in places like Corinth and Galatia, were wondering why they should listen to Paul at all. If he was really God's messenger, wouldn't he have a smoother path? Wouldn't he be a nicer guy? Wouldn't the "wins" be bigger and more obvious?

Paul was under no illusion about either himself or his friends. Clay jar was probably too subtle—more like cracked pot—or crackpot. But God had made this promise to the Christian community: *There is all-surpassing power at work within you. I put it there so that you can participate in what I am up to in this world. Do not be afraid. Use that power to do good and to share the good news.* (2 Cor. 4:7) And, at least on his good days, Paul believed it.

We're convinced that if this clay jar of a church has a future, it starts here. It starts now.

You can't use what you can't see

There is no missional leadership model, evangelistic program, emerging worship service, or anything else that is going to lead us into a new day. Only God, who is on the loose and at work in the world, reconciling creation and setting people free, can do that. And it frustrates us that, when it comes to believing in this God, so many church people we meet appear to be having more bad days than good ones.

On their really bad days, church folk are hard-hearted and crabby when somebody suggests they try doing things in a new way or risk going in a new direction. They can't—or won't—believe that God might be speaking to them through the new voices in their communities or the young voices in their midst. They make decisions and take actions that appear to completely contradict what they say they believe about the one who has called, gathered and sent them into mission. They let fear win.

One congregational member, attending a presentation we were making to a group of judicatory leaders, publically berated us at the end of our workshop. He wanted hard data that what we were teaching "works" and wanted a guarantee that, if the judicatory set us free to work with congregations in that territory, there would be significant numerical growth in membership.

He accused us of pulling a fast one with the intention of skipping town like Harold Hill (a.k.a. "The Music Man") without actually accomplishing anything of any value. The intensity and harshness of his tirade took us by surprise. What were we teaching that got this man so upset?

We told him that we didn't know of any strategy the church has tried over the past several decades that could fix the problems most congregations and denominations are facing today. But we are convinced the church is being called to follow God confidently, creatively and collaboratively into the emerging future.

We were teaching those leaders how to help people open up the Scriptures so they could listen together for that call. We were helping them learn to ask purposeful questions like *What in the world is God up to? What is God's purpose for us? What is God calling us to do?* And specifically, we were setting them free to wrestle with these questions in their own personal, everyday lives. We were honest when we said we didn't know what (if anything) could fix their churches, but that we were willing to walk with them as they learned how to be a part of what God is up to wherever they live, work, play, learn, worship and serve.

He just couldn't swallow it. He might have been willing to trust us if we were willing to make promises we couldn't keep—but he wasn't willing or able to trust God.

We don't often find ourselves on the front lines of people's frustration and fear like we were that day. But we see this kind of incredulity and mistrust at work in plenty of other places and ways. It usually happens when people are focused on what they are *not* and what they *don't* have, rather than on what God has done and is doing in their midst. It isn't necessarily that they don't believe in God. But they do have a hard time believing that God is at work in and through them. Perhaps they have just become so discouraged, anxious or burned out that they can no longer see God. They can't see the treasure of extraordinary power that dwells within them. All they can see is the clay jar. And you can't use what you can't see.

Jump on board

It saddens us that so many of our brothers and sisters in the church can't see that God is at work in and through them. It exasperates us because we know that God is on the move. From the word "Go!" (or even before) God has been on a mission, reconciling the whole creation and setting people free.

Go from the land of your ancestors to the land that I will give you, where you will be blessed so that, through you, all the people of the earth might be blessed. (Genesis 12:1-3)

Let my people go! (Exodus 5:1)

Go, learn what this means: I desire mercy, not sacrifice. (Matthew 9:13)

Go, show yourself to the priest. (Luke 5:14)

Go and tell what you have seen and heard. (Luke 7:22)

There is nothing static about the God we meet in the biblical story. This God is always doing something, always going somewhere, always calling, sending, healing, blessing, feeding, setting people free from whatever is choking the life out of them.

It is painfully true that humans, including (especially?) the most religious ones in the bunch, haven't always been very good at paying attention to what God is up to. Back in the old days they laughed at, scorned and ignored the prophets. So finally, God sent Jesus, who announced and accomplished what God had been promising all along.

Hey! Turn around and see what God has done. The kingdom is here! (Luke 17:21) Every single wall that you try to build to separate yourselves from God has been torn down. Every single wall that you try to build to separate yourselves from each other...double down. There is no distinction between Jew or Gentile, male or female, slave or free, rich or poor, gay or straight, black or brown or white. In Christ, all are made one. (Gal. 3:23-29)

Jesus got killed for saying things like this, but not even death could put an end to God's mission of reconciliation and freedom. The empty tomb was just another way of saying:

Nothing in all creation can ever separate you from God's love through Jesus Christ. Neither fear nor sin nor death. Neither angels nor rulers nor things present nor things to come. Neither hardship nor persecution nor sword. Not even your misguided attempt to kill God's love. Nothing. (Rom. 8:31-39)

Post-resurrection, God just kept doing what God has always done. Everybody got invited to the party. And everybody got a job:

Didn't you hear me? The walls have all come down. Now, go tell everyone you meet! Tell them what I have done and what I am doing. And above all, live like all of it is true. (Acts 1:8, Phil. 1:27)

It is maddening when church folk become so fixated on their deficiencies, disagreements, rituals, rules and whatever else distracts them that they miss out on what God has done and is doing; when they can't see it, when they don't say it and when they insist on acting like it never happened. We have heard God's mission described as a moving train.[9] And this train is leaving the station. It's time to jump on board.

We don't pretend to know what the future of the institutional church or your particular congregation will look like. We don't even know if the church of our emerging future will *have* congregations as they exist today, where people gather once a week in a building they own and are led by a 'professionally' trained pastor they've drafted from another team (i.e., congregation) or brought up from the minor leagues (i.e., academia).

We don't know what seminaries, judicatories, denominations or parachurch organizations will look like 100 or even 10 years from now; or if they will even exist in a way that will be recognizable to us.

But we are quite sure that God will work, as God has always done, in and through *people,* to bring reconciliation and freedom to the world God so loves. And we want to be ready for whatever that looks like. We suspect that you do, too.

Becoming a renewable church

Too many church folk are having too many bad days. But we believe there are even more people in the church today who are crying out like the father of the boy with convulsions (Mark 9:24), who grabbed Jesus by the robe and pleaded, *Lord, I believe! Help my unbelief!*

The question our team hears more than any other is this one: How?! How can we hear God speaking to us? How can we know what God is calling us to do? And how are we supposed to do anything about it? How can we possibly be useful to God's mission in the world when so many of us are struggling, divided, burned out and, in some cases, so very small? How can we be effective when everything around us is

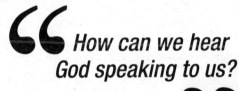

How can we hear God speaking to us?

changing so fast we never feel like we're on solid ground? How can we let go of *what was* and see *what is* for the sake of *what might be?* How can we get ready to follow God into this emerging future?

If any of these questions have ever crossed your mind, we want you to hear us clearly now: God, who is on a mission to reconcile the whole creation and set all people free, also wants you to live in the reconciliation and freedom that is yours.

It's got to be breaking God's heart to watch people in any organization, any community, any school, any business or any family waste away. Seriously. Each one of us has been made in the image of the Creator. We have been made to create. We were born to dream and to make something of those dreams using all the gifts and all the passion that is in us. When that energy, intelligence and imagination gets squandered, for whatever reason, it has to make God heartsick. When this happens in the church, we can only imagine the tears God sheds.

On a snowy day a few years back, we asked a roomful of religious leaders in the Upper Peninsula (a slice of Michigan, way up north, sandwiched between Lakes Michigan and Superior) to make a list of those things which characterize a healthy, vital congregation—the kind of place they'd like to work. "We'd all be willing to stand in the same ice shack[10] together!" one of them blurted out. And the list grew from there.

"People take the initiative," someone said. "There's no grapevine!" somebody else shouted out. "There is healthy communication." "People are willing to try new things!" "They can disagree maturely." "There is a permission-giving culture. People know their gifts and are encouraged to use them." "There is a vision beyond survival."

Then we asked the group, "How many of you work in a place like this?" Not a single person raised a hand. Not one.[11]

This is not the kind of church God had in mind. And it's not the kind of world God has in mind either. We don't believe it has to be this way in *any* organization. We are convinced that the most resilient and adaptable organizations in this new century will be those in which people figure out a new way—a *renewable* way—to do work and life together.

A renewable organization taps and unleashes the energy that is within it and therefore is always ready for whatever changes the future brings. People who can *be who they are and use what they have to do what matters* are not afraid of what tomorrow will be like. Instead of dwelling on what they don't have and letting fear prevent them from trying new things, leaders set people free to imagine and innovate, experiment and engage.

The old hierarchies that might have made sense when Henry Ford rolled that first automobile off the assembly line are flattened so that no one's intelligence or energy goes to waste. And those organizations that can't or won't let go of those old ways of working together will find themselves becoming toxic; as poisonous to people as they are to the planet. In fact, we think those two things are related.[12]

Archbishop Desmond Tutu agrees. He is a South African church leader and social activist who won a Nobel Peace Prize for his work toward bringing an end to apartheid in the 1980s. Over the past several decades, he has raised his voice in defense of human rights across the globe and to fight AIDS, poverty, racism and homophobia. In 2005, he received the Gandhi Peace Prize. He has spent his life working on behalf of people, especially the poor and vulnerable, because he believes that we all belong to one family—the human family. He believes that our planet is in peril because, very simply, humans have forgotten the basic connection we have to each other. We have been irresponsible stewards of the earth, engaging in reckless consumerism and slurping up the planet's natural resources. We have forgotten our moral obligation to care for one another. Today the results are being felt most severely by the poor, who suffer most from the impact of drought, high temperatures, flooding and unpredictable weather events resulting from climate change. "We must act now," he writes. We must remember our responsibility to each other, especially to the poor and marginalized, and that will mean making sure the planet is healthy enough to support and sustain us all. In other words, Tutu says, "Once we start living in a way that is people-friendly to all of God's family, we will also be environment-friendly." [13]

The future of life and work in every organization, including the church, is both planet-friendly *and* people-friendly. Thankfully, there all kinds of voices out there today, across a variety of disciplines, helping us figure out how to get there.[14] They are helping us find our way; a poignant reminder that God is on the loose in the world. Their work has informed our own as we have developed the practices and principles of The Renewable Organization.

But there is one voice above all others leading us into this emerging future, challenging us to stop treating the planet and her people like they are disposable, teaching us how to tap into and unleash the treasure of extraordinary power that dwells within us, calling us to use that power for good no matter what tomorrow brings. It is because we have heard this one voice that all of these other voices sound so familiar and so compelling. We heard it first from Jesus.

Looking for God...

...through the biblical story:

1 Corinthians 1:18-31
If you're in a small group, read the passage out loud.

Paul is talking to a group of Christians who have been arguing about who has the stronger faith and the most spiritual gifts; they have taken sides against each other, some following Paul, others following Peter, etc. Paul reminds them that Christianity isn't a race to the top of the heap; God has always chosen the most unlikely people to work with and through to get things done.

1. In what way would you describe your faith community or organization as a "clay jar" or a "cracked pot?" What difference does it make to know that even the very first faith communities—the ones you read about in the Bible—were clay jars, too?

2. How do you think the people Paul was writing to felt about being reminded that they were, after all, a bunch of people who weren't very smart, powerful or wealthy? Why do you think he risked saying this to them?

3. Who do you know who is "foolish," "weak" or "despised" by the world, whom God has used to do something really amazing and wonderful? What kind of impact did they have? What's the story?

1. Do you believe there is a treasure of "all-surpassing power" at work within you, in your own everyday life? Where have you seen evidence of it? When have you felt God working through you to make a difference in somebody else's life?

2. Where have you seen God's "all-surpassing power" at work in your faith community or organization? How is God working through you, as a group, to make a difference in people's lives and the world?

3. Where have you noticed fear taking hold in your faith community or organization? Why do you think this is? What do you think people are afraid of? How is fear holding you back from doing what you think you should be doing, as a faith community or organization? What else is holding you back?

4. What do you think about the idea that no one really knows what the "emerging future" (including the future of your faith community or organization) looks like? Do you think this idea is frightening? Or does it set you free?

5. What do you think people in your faith community or organization may have to "let go of" in order to see "what might be"?

1. List three words that describe the faith community or organization you're a part of. What three words do you think the people in your neighbourhood, community and/or service area would use to describe your faith community or organization? What reflections do you have about that? What do you hear God saying to you about that?

2. God is already on a mission—bringing reconciliation and freedom to people in the world, including in your community. What is God doing "out there" in your context that you haven't noticed before? What is happening in your neighbourhood, town, etc. that looks like it has God's "fingerprints" all over it? What would it look like if you decided to jump in and help?

The Back Story

[9] We can't be sure, but we think we first heard this image used by the great 20th century missionary and missiologist, Lesslie Newbigin.

[10] A portable shelter fishermen build on the ice over the fishing hold they've drilled. They sit in the shelter while they're fishing to keep warm even on the coldest days. (We had to ask, too.)

[11] This story first appeared in Kelly Fryer's article "Creative outreach: how's it going where you are?" *The Lutheran*, April 2005.

[12] This link between how people are treated and how the planet is treated has not been taken very seriously in the past. But that is changing. For the first time, in March 2008, the United Nations Human Rights Council passed a resolution on human rights and climate change that calls on the Office of the High Commissioner of Human Rights to undertake "a detailed analytical study of the relationship between climate change and human rights" for consideration by the Council (See UN Doc. A/HRC/7/L.21/Rev.1 [26 March 2008]. That same year The International Council on Human Rights Policy issued a document called Climate Change and Human Rights: A Rough Guide. Writing in the forward, Mary Robinson, who is the President of Realizing Rights: The Ethical Globalization Initiative, argues that the connection between how the planet gets treated and how people get treated is so very clear that environmental abuse ought to be considered a convictable human rights offense. There is good reason, she says, to consider viewing the environmental crisis primarily through the lens of human rights. Why? Robinson writes: "The human rights framework reminds us that climate change is about suffering—about the human misery that results directly from the damage we are doing to nature." (Climate Change and Human Rights: A Rough Guide, 2008, 2008 International Council on Human Rights Policy [48, chemin du Grand-Montfleury, P. O. Box 147, 1290 Versoix, Switzerland])

[13] This quote is from Tutu's introduction to *The Green Bible*, (New York: HarperCollins Publishers. 2008).

[14] Some of the most helpful, we think, are working in the field of social innovation at places like Social Innovation Generation at Waterloo, Ontario, and the Center for Social Innovation at Stanford. Symbolic-interpretive and postmodern organization theorists like Mary Jo Hatch and Margaret Wheatley, and contemporary management gurus like MIT's Thomas Malone, are making strong research-based arguments for decentralization in the workplace and beyond as both the preferred and the inevitable future.

An Invitation To Freedom

"Follow me, and I will make you fish for people." — Matthew 4:19

When Jesus called his first disciples, it was a big clue that God was going to keep doing what God had always done. God works in and through people to bring reconciliation and freedom to the world. But the invitation Jesus gave to those guys on the beach that day is a pivotal one in more ways than one. This story, especially the way Matthew (4:18-22) tells it, frames, in a clear way, the nature of the relationship into which each one of us is being called. And it gives a picture of how Jesus expects us to live and work together as we participate in God's mission in the world. In this story we catch a glimpse of what a *renewable* church might look like.

We have to guess a little about the context of this story because the author doesn't give us much to go on. But we know these guys were living in occupied territory. Their government was a sham; the local ruler had been hand-picked by and was a puppet of a foreign power. They were not only taxed without representation, their money was used to support the regime that oppressed them. They were free to worship in their own manner and keep their customs, but that was at the whim of their subjugator. The enemy's army patrolled their streets. Imagine life on the 17th century slave coast, or as an 18th century Native American, a 19th century Catholic in Ireland, or a 20th century Parisian under Nazi occupation. Think modern day Afghanistan, Pakistan, Darfur. This may be a little harsh, but we hope you're starting to get the picture.

Long ago, their prophets had warned the ancestors of those Jewish fishermen (and ours) that this time would come. They tried to cajole the people into a return to faithfulness, to remind them of their core values, to turn them back towards God and neighbour. But they would not listen. Their laziness and lack of focus made them an easy mark. When the Romans marched in, the people didn't even put up a fight.

But they were weary of this life. They were sick of impoverishment, of feeling like they never had enough, and they were tired of powerlessness. They longed for a return to greatness. They sang about the great kings of ancient times and dreamed of the one to come who would be their salvation. In short, they were hoping for a bailout. What they got, instead, was Jesus.

Better than a bailout

Unlike those ancient fishermen, most people we know aren't looking for a saviour to deliver them from political oppression. That's just not our context. But there are many people we know who wish Jesus would show up to save their churches. You can't blame them. There's a ton of stuff wrong with some churches today. People in small churches are often worried and scared and sick of feeling powerless and poor. Even people who belong to big congregations with a lot of people and a lot of money aren't immune from feeling nervous and getting tired; it takes a ton of work to keep those gynormous places going after all.

But Jesus isn't the candy man. Remember the old song from the "Willie Wonka and the Chocolate Factory" 1971 film soundtrack? Some of you might even remember when Sammy Davis, Jr.'s cover the following year, which hit #1 on the Billboard Hot 100 Chart, made it even more famous. The candy man can do anything. He can take a sunrise and sprinkle it in dew, make the sun into a strawberry lemon pie, and dip tomorrow in a dream. Why? Because he mixes everything with love and makes the world taste good, that's why! Gene Wilder's candy man in the movie turned out to be a lot stranger and even a little scary. But that doesn't stop folks from wishing the candy man was real. And that, for a lot of people (and maybe for all of us sometimes) is where Jesus comes in.

He forgives my sins! He cures me when I'm sick! He fixes my broken relationships! He helps me sell my house in a bad market! He finds me parking spots in those crowded shopping mall lots! I bet he can even fix my church!

Notice how this candy man Jesus is all about…*me*. We're not saying this wouldn't be nice. It just isn't how the story goes. It was clear right from the start that Jesus wasn't bringing a bailout. As much as those fishermen and their friends might have wanted it, Jesus wasn't offering the renewal of their fortunes or a return to some gilded past. He wasn't even promising a glorious tomorrow—at least not the way they might have imagined it. They probably couldn't be blamed for not understanding this right away. And they didn't understand—not until after the whole death and resurrection operation. Jesus had to explain it again and again. Recall the meddling mother of James and John who asked Jesus to put her boys at his side, one on the right and one on the left, when he finally made his move for the throne. How many times did he have to say it?

Jesus doesn't come to fix our problems or grant our wishes. He comes with something even better than that. He comes with an invitation to follow him on a life-changing, world-shaking adventure. Jesus invites each one of us to be a part of what God is up to in the world, to step out into unknown waters for the sake of other people and the planet we share. Jesus comes with an invitation to freedom. Because it's Jesus who extends the invitation, of course, it sounds an awful lot like a call. You know right away this isn't something you should ignore and you better think about it long and hard before you turn it down. But why would you want to anyway?

The call to be a part of what God is up to is a great gift. It is what gives life meaning and purpose. It doesn't always make you happy. In fact, answering this call usually requires hard work and sacrifice. But it can and does produce real joy. Responding to God's claim on your life opens your eyes to the way in which, through the things you say and do, God is reconciling the whole creation and setting people free. Once you've experienced it, you'll wonder how you ever lived without it.

Who do you know that is answering that call today? Seriously. Who do you know that resists the temptation to turn Jesus into their own personal genie in a bottle and instead understands the gift they have been given as a call to serve others, to do justice, to love tenderly, to walk

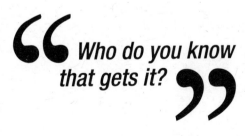

Who do you know that gets it?

humbly, to pay attention to what God is up to and jump in to help in whatever way they can? Who do you know that *gets* it? Put this book down right now and send them an email or a Tweet, write on their Facebook wall, call them on the phone, or drop them a note. Thank them for being an example of what it means to have a backbone, to be a Christian, to answer the call.

Everybody's invited

Jesus wasn't exactly breaking new ground when he invited those fishermen to come along on his adventure. The biblical story introduces a God whose loving mission to bless, reconcile, save and set free is at least as old as creation. All throughout this story God invites people to participate in this mission. And, to be perfectly honest, they aren't exactly the most qualified bunch. A couple of nomadic retirees named Abram and Sarai are tapped to start a family, through which people all over the world would hear about the God who loves them and wants them to love each other (Genesis 12:1-3). A man with a stutter and an unsavoury past is recruited to convince the most powerful ruler on earth that he should tell his dirt-cheap workforce, "Go on, get outta here. I'm setting you free." Ever since then, the story of how Moses brought Pharaoh to his knees has inspired people living in every kind of bondage to make a break for freedom (Exodus).

A couple thousand years later, an unwed teenage mother becomes a vessel for bearing God's own presence into the world (Luke 2).

Jesus provides the best cliffhanger of an ending ever conceived when he gives a couple of fishermen, an accountant and a woman (gasp!) the job of carrying the most important message ever to the ends of the earth (Matthew 28).

God never works alone. And God loves to tap the most unlikely people for the job.

Some of the leaders we know who are risking new ways of being and doing church wear torn up jeans and funky glasses, meet for "worship" in a coffeehouse or a bar, cover themselves with tattoos and txt 2 b heard. But a lot of people we know who are daring to answer Jesus' call are, well, a lot more ordinary than that. Take, for example, the bunch of Lutherans in the Manitoba-Northwestern Ontario Synod of the Evangelical Lutheran Church in Canada we met in Dauphin.

Dauphin is about a four-hour drive from Winnipeg, Manitoba, through some of the flattest terrain you've ever seen. The reason our team made this journey was to present a day long learning event for congregational leaders who had gathered for a rather quixotic annual convention.

We don't usually write by name about the people and organizations we're working with at A Renewal Enterprise, Inc. Our friends, clients and partners can count on us to maintain their confidentiality. But we asked for (and got!) permission to share the story of what happened that weekend because, well, it's just such a good example of the kind of brave and wacky things ordinary church leaders are willing to do when they realize they've been invited to be a part of Jesus' great adventure.

When they were planning for this event the leadership team, in a bold moment, decided to put their words about being committed to rural folk and their communities into action by choosing this out of the way place to gather.

Most of the 150 or so delegates came by bus from Winnipeg (where most people in the synod actually live). It took all of the Lutheran churches in the area, together with their friends and neighbours from other denominations, working together to pull off the event. The convention was held in the church building of the United Church congregation in town because none of the Lutherans had a big enough building. The banquet was hosted and served by the people of the Ukrainian Church down the road, who also provided the evening's entertainment in the form of traditional Ukrainian dancing. The roadside motel where most of the delegates stayed (one of the few if not the only real lodging option in Dauphin) was packed out. The motel manager was so excited he kept the motel pool open until midnight each evening in order to accommodate the group, a mild-mannered but merry band if you ever saw one. On Sunday morning, during the final worship service, the whole crowd packed into the small Lutheran church building in town and sat shoulder to shoulder with the members of that congregation…folks who had been our gracious hosts all weekend long.

Our guess is that the folks in Dauphin will remember this event forever. The weekend they hosted the convention of the MNO Synod will be written down in their history books, right along with building projects, special anniversaries and their roster of those who have served as pastor. Everybody who experienced being honoured guests in this little town will remember it, too.

The thing is, this was an expensive project, in a bunch of ways. Several people were overheard wondering out loud if this was the best use of what sometimes feels like scarce funds. Even the planners had to be a little worried that this was a big mistake. Not only had they chosen an unusual location, they had changed the whole structure of the convention. Instead of day after long day of "business," they did their work in a single day and spent the rest of their time in prayer, Bible study and holy conversation about what in the world God is up to. They asked purposeful questions about what it means to be a church in mission for others. And they learned some things they can do 'back home' to help their congregations engage in this same kind of process. And they had a lot of fun doing it.

In all kinds of ways, this was a risky thing for the leaders of this synod to do. But by the end of the event, our hunch is that evaluations said something like this: We're not sure about transporting the whole synod convention across the province next year but this…this was *awesome*.

Now, we know this much is true: Changing up the way they did convention that year didn't add a single new member to a single congregation in that synod. At least, as far as we know. It didn't solve the problem of membership decline or shrinking funds. It didn't suddenly turn each one gathered into an enthusiastic evangelist. It didn't put a stop to the rural despair so many living in Manitoba and Northwestern Ontario experience.

It was not without risk. But it *was* different. It brought hope, fellowship and tangible help (Just imagine how many dollars got pumped into that little local economy by all those happy Lutherans.) to people who most of the time feel like they live on the edge of the world (Actually, they kind of do.) It happened because a couple busloads of church leaders had a feeling that God was up to something out there…and they wanted to go find out what it was.

Really, you don't have to be on the cutting edge of anything to imagine being and doing church in a new way. You can jump on board just as you are, whenever and wherever you see God at work. You can suit up to confront the windmills/giants/challenges of this age right where you live, with exactly the gifts God has given you, even if you find yourself in a place like Dauphin, 300 km northwest of Winnipeg.

No more excuses

When Jesus ran into those guys on the beach, he didn't ask for their credentials. He wasn't interested in where they had gone to school or who was on their list of references or whether they had ever done anything worthy of a recommendation. You might argue that Jesus could somehow mysteriously peer into their souls and see that one day they'd turn out to be great leaders. But there isn't anything in the story, as Matthew tells it, to indicate that Jesus even gave it much thought. Besides, these guys turned out to have a pretty mixed record when it came to doing the stuff Jesus asked them to do. They were the poster boys for clay jars. And let's not even mention Judas.

No, we think it's fair to say that Jesus didn't invite these guys to be a part of what God is up to because they deserved it. Jesus' call came to them as a gift. There wasn't anything they had to say, do or be to earn it; it came without condition. Jesus knew he was getting a mixed bag (at best). And so, when he said *come follow me,* it also meant *you are loved! You are set free from worrying that you are not! You are free from sin, death, shame, self-doubt and anything else that might prevent you from loving God and serving your neighbour!*

And that's how the call comes to each one of us. This is ironic, of course, because one of the most enduring debates in most (if not all) faith communities is about who is entitled to belong and, even more often, who is qualified to lead.

You can see evidence that the very earliest Christians tussled over the issue of membership in Paul's letters and in the Book of Acts, which tells about the beginnings of the Church. As the story goes, Peter and the leaders in Jerusalem wanted the Christian community to remain exclusively Jewish (Gal. 2:7-14). Paul, Timothy, Priscilla and others who were working to spread the message about Jesus beyond the Jewish capital city discerned that God's love and freedom were intended for all people, regardless of cultural, political, social, economic, religious or any other kind of distinction (Rom. 3:22-24). They also sparred over who could lead. The original eleven apostles, after they lost Judas to whatever demons possessed him, replaced him with a man (naturally) who had been "with Jesus from the beginning" (Acts 1:21-23). They couldn't have foreseen and weren't very happy at first when Paul, a former enemy, started claiming that he was an apostle, too, appointed by Jesus himself (Gal. 1:11-24). We can't know for sure but they probably weren't thrilled when Paul started putting women in charge of the churches he planted, either (1 Cor. 16:1-7). This is an age-old issue and it's not over yet.

In the summer of 2009, after many years of internal struggles that sometimes spilled over into the public square, former President Jimmy Carter announced that he was severing his ties with the Southern Baptist Convention after a lifetime of membership and service within that community of faith. Why? Because of his view that their policies regarding the role of women in the family, in society and in the church are not only wrong, but they contribute to unspeakable damage to the lives of girls and women around the world.

Carter wrote, "...my decision to sever my ties with the Southern Baptist Convention, after six decades, was painful and difficult. It was, however, an unavoidable decision when the convention's leaders, quoting a few carefully selected Bible verses and claiming that Eve was created second to Adam and was responsible for original sin, ordained that women must be 'subservient' to their husbands and prohibited from serving as deacons, pastors or chaplains in the military service. This was in conflict with my belief—confirmed in the holy scriptures—that we are all equal in the eyes of God."[15]

The poet Robert Frost famously wrote in his poem *"Mending Wall"*:

*Something there is
that doesn't love a wall,
That wants it down.*

But it seems to us also true that there's something about people that makes us want to build a wall out of whatever pile of stones happens to be lying around. How else do you explain all the hurdles that get constructed to keep certain people in and certain people out? How else to understand the piles of rules and regulations about who can preach or teach or baptize or set the Lord's Table? How else to make sense of the walls you may have built in your own mind that make you think you aren't worthy of the call Jesus has given to you? *I'm too young. I'm too old. I'm not smart enough. I'm not charismatic enough. I'm not brave enough.*

Enough, already! Jesus' call doesn't come to you because you deserve or earn it. Maybe he sees something in you that you can't see yourself. But it's more likely that it just doesn't matter if something remarkable or amazing is there to see or not. Jesus' call comes to you because, well, he just can't seem to help himself. There are no more excuses.

You means you

We think the story about Jesus' call to those fishermen on the beach is helpful in a lot of ways. But it can also be a pain in the neck. The words Jesus spoke to those guys have inspired bumper stickers, T-shirts, posters and countless Christian knick-knacks. "Gone fishin'!" they say. Or something like it. But frankly we think the whole 'fishing' thing as an image for evangelism or mission has created huge troubles for Christians (and the rest of the world) over the centuries. When you understand your job to be 'reeling people in' for Christ, you end up treating people like objects, even if you don't mean it that way. They become things to be conquered and consumed. Seriously, what happens after you catch a big one? You fry it up and eat it with a side of boiled potatoes. No wonder so many people think Christians are scary.

In order for this story to be helpful, you need to remember that 'fishing' is what he called those *fishermen* to do. It isn't what Jesus calls *us* to do. It isn't even what he called Matthew (Mat.9:9-13—the tax collector and the guy tradition says is behind this Gospel story) or Mary Magdalene (Mat. 28:1-10) to do. When Jesus told those fishermen he was going to teach them how to fish for people, he wasn't delivering a great new commandment or speaking in code about some kind of universal and timeless evangelism strategy. He was inviting them— *them!*—a couple of bruised up, weather-beaten fishermen, to be a part of what God is up to. And that didn't mean they had to become something or someone different than who they already were. He didn't, for example, tell them they had to be great preachers or teachers or even carpenters. He asked them to be exactly who they were...*fishermen*. And, the way we read this story, he invited them to use exactly what they had to work with...*their nets and their boats*...to make a difference in the world.

It's true, the author of this story does say that when these guys heard Jesus say *come follow me* they immediately left their nets and their boats behind. But we're also told that it wasn't long (Mat. 8:18) before Jesus and the disciples were getting into those boats to escape the crowds. As a matter of fact, Jesus and the disciples were always getting into and out of a boat. Jesus used those boats to teach from when the crowds were really big; the water was a natural projection system (Lk. 5:3). He used those boats to cross more quickly from one side of the lake to the other, to get to the people who needed him (Lk. 8:22-23). He used those boats just to get away from it all once in awhile. Jesus *needed* those boats. In fact, we don't know for sure, but our guess is that the story went something like this: When Jesus looked back and saw those two fishermen following him, with their nets and their boats becoming smaller and smaller dots on the horizon, he said *What are you guys doing?! Are you nuts or something?! Go back there and get that stuff. We're going to need it!*

The point is, when Jesus invites you to follow him, he invites you to *be who you are and see what you have for the sake of doing what matters* to God. "You" really means *you*. Jesus' call to follow him is an invitation to freedom. There is nothing you need to be, earn, buy, build or acquire in order to be useful to God. There is no need for fear, embarrassment, anxiety or shame. You can't be too old or too young, too rich or too poor. There is no such thing as inadequate. Jesus sees you, knows you, calls you, and is setting you free to put exactly who you are and what you have into the service of God's loving mission.

Looking for God...

...through the biblical story:

Luke 5:1-11
If you're in a small group, read the passage out loud.

This is another version of the story about Jesus calling the first disciples. In this story, Jesus doesn't just suggest that he might need their boats one day, he actually uses one.

1. What else do you notice about this story? What jumps out at you? What are you hearing God say to you through this story?

2. Jesus calls the disciples to "put out into the deep water." In what way is God calling you to do that today? Where is the "deep water" for you? Where is the "deep water" for your faith community or organization? If you're hesitating over casting your nets into "deep water," name what's holding you back.

3. When the fishermen listened to Jesus, their nets overflowed! They needed help to pull them in. When have you and/or your faith community or organization answered Jesus' call to do something new? In what way did your nets begin to overflow? Who had an opportunity to join in because you suddenly had your hands full and needed help? What else happened?

...through each other:

1. Can you think of a time in your personal life or in your shared life and work, when you thought of Jesus as "the candy man"? What happened? What would have happened if Jesus had granted all your wishes and made "the world taste good"? If Jesus isn't the candy man who makes all your dreams come true, what is he good for?! What does Jesus mean to you? What difference does he make in your life and in your life together?

2. List all the people you know who understand that the gift they have been given is a call to serve others; to do justice, to love tenderly, to walk humbly, to pay attention to what God is up to and to jump in to help in whatever way they can. Share the story of one of these people. And, over the next two weeks, take a moment to contact each one of the people on your list and thank them for bearing the Good News to you through their actions.

3. Are there people in your faith community or organization whose gifts and passions are being ignored, wasted or even rejected because they don't look like "good Christians" or "good leaders" are supposed to look?

4. What would your organization look like if everyone's gifts were being put to good use? What can you do about that?

5. What do you think about the idea that *there is nothing you need to be, earn, buy, build or acquire in order to be useful to God…you can't be too old, young, rich, poor, etc.?* Does the idea that there are "no more excuses" make you feel free, or nervous, or something else? Why?

...through your neighbour:

1. Are there walls between people in your context (e.g. your neighbourhood, city, wider community) that need to come down? If so, what are they? What can you do about that?

2. Do you agree that the image of "fishing for people" has been an unhelpful way to describe our job as Christians? Why or why not? What reaction do you think our non-Christian neighbours have when they hear Christians use this image? What do you think about the idea that Jesus isn't calling you to "fish for people" but is, instead, calling you to *be who you are and see what you have for the sake of doing what matters?*

The Back Story

[15] Jimmy Carter, "The Words of God Do Not Justify Cruelty to Women," *The Observer*, July 12, 2009.

Making the Shift

"...What you are doing is not good. You will surely wear yourself out, both you and these people with you." Exodus 18:17-18a

How often do you hear the people you work with play the 'fill-in-the-blank' game? If you don't know what we're talking about, it goes something like this: You're in a meeting and people are brainstorming and there's pretty good energy but it's starting to fade because somebody in the room keeps coming up with reasons why one idea after another just won't work. And the worst thing is he's right. Then someone else says, wistfully:

If we only had _____, we could do (whatever it is we want to do/need to do/think we're supposed to do).

And the conversation is over.

This 'fill-in-the-blank' game is just one characteristic of what we're calling a *consumable* approach to life and work. This is the predominant approach in most organizations (including faith-based ones) today. The result is that you feel like you never have enough of anything. The whole focus of your life and work becomes whatever is in the blank. You set up command-and-control systems, putting somebody in charge of telling everybody else what to do and how to do it, to make sure you get that blank filled as quickly and efficiently as possible. And the only reason whatever is in the blank is important is because of what it has the potential to produce for you. Your metric of success isn't *what difference did I make in the world today?* You're not wondering *did I make a contribution to something or somebody else?* You're not thinking *how are we being useful to God?* All you're focused on is that thing in the blank; how to get it, what it can do for you and what a disaster it'll be if you don't get it. In this consumable approach to life and work, the metrics of success become *did I get it? What did it do for me? Did I get what I wanted out of it?* And it doesn't matter what the 'it' is, either. It could be a natural resource. It could be a building or a parking lot. It could be a new staff person or a new church member (preferably the <u>tithing</u>, <u>volunteering</u>, <u>non-complaining</u> kind). On the other hand, not being able to fill in the blank with enough money or people or whatever is debilitating. It leaves you feeling impotent and powerless. For a lot of church folk today, not being able to fill in the blank has become *The Great Excuse* to throw up their hands in despair and do nothing.

No wonder the planet is so messed up. No wonder so many people feel like the life is being sucked out of them by their job. No wonder people say they're burned out by church.

That story about the call to his first disciples illustrates that Jesus has shown us a different way:

- **Be who you are;**
- **See what you have;**
- **Do what matters.**

We call this a *renewable* approach to life and work because it is in such stark contrast to the *consumable* way most people are functioning today. Making the shift is not going to be easy. But it should not be hard to see why this shift is necessary for any organization (including the church) that expects to thrive in the emerging future. All across Canada and the U.S. we are seeing this consumable culture come tumbling down.

The end of an era

The *Great Recession* that began in the last half of the first decade of the 21st century hasn't really been nice to anybody, even to those institutions that seemed 'too big to fail.' Take Harvard University, for example; with a pre-crash endowment of nearly $37 billion, Harvard was the richest university in the world—or so everyone thought. Truth is the Harvard administration and board spent and borrowed so much money over the past decade on new construction, planning for a new campus, new land purchases, new faculty positions, new financial aid programs, and 'general bureaucracy creep' that post-crash they have found themselves in a hole so big no one is quite sure how they're going to climb out. An estimated drop of $11 billion in the value of the endowment has left the university with insufficient funds to support their debt or pay their bills. "We are in trouble," said one Crimson professor. In the aftermath of deep and damaging cuts, he speculated, "There is a real chance that Harvard will no longer be considered the best there is."[16] Some folks may want to argue about whether or not Harvard is or ever was the "best," but there's no question it's in trouble now. One observer is more descriptive: "Radical change is coming to Harvard. Fewer professors, for one thing. Fewer teaching assistants, janitors and support staff. Shuttered libraries. Less money for research and travel and books. Cafés replaced by vending machines. Junior-varsity sports teams downgraded to clubs. No raises. No bonuses. No fresh coats of paint or new carpets. Overflowing trash cans."[17] There are even reports the thermostats are being turned down to save money in the winter.

We don't know enough of the back story to agree that "the same lethal mix of uncurbed expansion, colossal debt, arrogance and mismanagement that ravaged Wall Street"[18] is to blame for what's happening at Harvard University these days. But we do know that what appears to have happened at Harvard is not unlike what we see in many other organizations, albeit on a much larger scale: Bad decisions made by people who have taken a consumable approach to their work. The mantra is "more." Their metric of success is disconnected from their purpose. In fact, they forget who they are and what really matters to them and what it is they were hoping to achieve. They take unnecessary risks. They make a mess. And the next thing you know everybody has to wear a parka to the office.

Some of the most influential scholars, researchers and leaders in the business world today have declared that we have "reached the limits of Management 1.0—the industrial age paradigm built atop the principles of standardization, specialization, hierarchy, control, and primacy of shareholder interests. [We] must face the fact that tomorrow's business imperatives lay outside the performance envelope of today's bureaucracy-infused management practices."[19]

In other words, no one really knows what they're doing when it comes to leading organizations today. But everybody does know that something new is needed. The world has shifted beneath our feet. The future is uncertain. The present is the story of one disaster after another. It's time to try something different.

The economic crisis that has shaken North America and much of the rest of the world is a signal that the time has come to shift from a consumable to a renewable way of living and working together. But this is not just an economic issue. Making this shift is not about saving the institutions on Wall Street or

Main Street or even on Church Street. This is a stewardship issue; it is a moral issue. A consumable culture is bad for the planet and for people. It is not the way God wants us to live and work together. The gifts, passions, assets, talents and abilities of too many people in too many places are being squandered. Lives are being wasted. It is time to learn what it means to be renewable, not just in the way we steward our natural resources, but also in the way we work and live together.

Taking your temperature

Although we don't know exactly what shape your faith community will take in the emerging future, we are pretty sure that you won't have a future unless you learn to live and work in a renewable way, leaving behind the practices and structures of the consumable approach most church leaders are using today. How do you know when you're acting out of a consumable model of ministry? What are the symptoms of a consumable approach in the church? Recognizing them may help you prevent a Harvard Yard-size disaster. It's a good first step towards making the shift from a consumable to a renewable church. Do you see yourself on this list?

- **It's harder and harder to find willing workers**
- **People don't show up for stuff. When they do they're crabby**
- **Turf wars**
- **Money wars**
- **Worship wars**
- **Burnout**
- **Backbiting and gossip**
- **People feel like what they're doing doesn't matter**
- **People feel like their voices aren't heard**

And the most serious symptom of all is this one:
- **People are turned in on themselves**

How is your faith community or organization doing? Maybe you're on death's doorstep. Or maybe you just have a little fever. But these symptoms, to one extent or another, are common in most churches today.

According to research done in one mainstream denomination, 43% of congregational members say they spend zero volunteer hours apart from their congregation's programs to help people in need or to make their own community a better place to live. 47% say they spend zero volunteer hours in their congregation to help people in need or to make their community a better place to live. And a whopping 67% of pastors say they spend two hours or less per week involved in community issues or organizations beyond the congregation.

This lack of interest or engagement with their community isn't because people are just so involved in running their congregations, either. This same survey reported that nearly 50% of congregational members say they are not involved *at all* in making decisions in their congregation…and most of them don't care. And less than one-third say their congregation has a clear vision and goals that they're personally committed to. Is it any wonder so many of our leaders are burnt out, discouraged and just a little bit cynical? Over a third of pastors surveyed say they feel lonely or isolated very or fairly often. Fewer than one-quarter are satisfied with their spiritual life. And nearly half say they have thought at least a little about leaving the ministry altogether.[20]

What do you think? Is there a problem? We would argue that, in fact, there is. And it isn't the kind of problem you can tweak your way out of, either.

You can't just 'fill-in-the-blank' with happier helpers by scheduling an annual Volunteer Appreciation Sunday or with more committed members by preaching a great sermon series telling everyone, in a classic command-and-control move, what the vision and goals of your congregation are. The fact that you might be tempted to think you could tweak your way out of this mess by filling in the blank with this, that or the other thing is just one more bit of evidence that there is a big problem. What we're

This is a moral issue

seeing can't be fixed by tweaking. There is a kind of toxic waste that infects many (most?) congregations, denominations and faith-based institutions today. It has been caused by decades (and maybe even centuries) of doing ministry within a consumable model.

Just think about the last annual report your congregation had to fill out. What are the metrics of success it used? Did it measure the things that really matter to you? Changed lives, maybe? Bellies fed? Authentic relationships developed within the congregation? Meaningful partnerships with people in your community? More composting, less waste? Most likely you were asked to measure the stuff that just fills in the blank: the number of bucks in the offering plate and butts in the pews. The kinds of things you'd maybe measure if you were running a 19th century factory, but not much that's connected to God's mission to reconcile the whole creation and set people free.

In this consumable church, your real purpose gets lost and it's replaced by something else. Usually, let's be honest now, that something else is getting people in the doors and convincing them to open their wallet—Period. People feel used. Leaders feel abused. And all of that extraordinary power that dwells within us goes to waste. Yes, there is indeed a problem.

The context of this crisis

The problem we're describing in the church is connected to a much larger crisis in organizational climate that is afflicting businesses, schools, agencies and every other kind of organization in North America today. It has to do with the models we've been using to live and work together, with the things we choose to measure, the way we have monetized natural resources, the way decisions get made and the role of leadership. This organizational climate crisis and the environmental climate crisis the planet is facing have a common starting point.

If you have a time machine, set the dial to right around the early 1900s. With Henry Ford's new car, horse and buggies were quickly becoming *so* yesterday. The craftsman, who took pride in creating by hand products that would be passed down from generation to generation, was suddenly an endangered species. The pace of life was quickening. The increasingly unquenchable thirst for "stuff" of all kinds was being matched by an inventive spirit and entrepreneurial drive never before seen in human history. And Ford was convinced that there had to be a better, quicker, cheaper way to get one of his automobiles into the garage of every single American. He was right.

Throughout the nineteenth and twentieth centuries, titans of industry like Mr. Ford built complex systems and accomplished remarkable levels of productivity and efficiency, delivering more products to more markets with greater speed than ever before. Generating clothing and food manufacturing, engineering, and chemical, iron and steel processing, the factory system required complex processes. Management learned to command-and-control. Bureaucracy swelled to meet the need of rapidly expanding social systems. The achievements of this period were, in fact, revolutionary. But it was not without its downside.

These factories burned up and guzzled down the earth's natural resources and they used people like they were disposable too. Workers, who were forced to specialize in routine, usually monotonous and quantifiably measurable tasks, became virtually interchangeable and easily replaceable. People, in other words, became little more than cogs in these elaborate machines. In Mr. Ford's factories, for example, it was against company policy to laugh on the job. If you were laughing, you were probably goofing off. And if you were goofing off, you were stealing from the company. Get caught smiling; get fired.[21]

These old factories and the bureaucratic systems that emerged to support them have left us with a powerful and mixed legacy. Nobody we know wants to dial back the time machine in order to actually *live* back before the Industrial Revolution gave us all the comforts of modern life. We certainly don't. But there has been a price to pay for those conveniences.

In a real sense, the way we're doing things together at work, in our schools and governmental agencies, in our non-profit organizations and yes, even in our faith communities, is for the most part still fundamentally based on the organizational models that developed during that era. Instead of authentic relationships between human beings who live and work together, both the planet and its people are still mainly "things" to be used until they're used up. It's okay to "drill, baby, drill" because everybody figures that, by the time our natural resources are finally depleted, it'll be somebody else's problem. And, in order to make sure it all gets done as efficiently as possible, somewhere in most organizations there is still a guy (or, in a few cases, a woman) sitting in a big office, earning a bigger salary than anybody else who is responsible for commanding and controlling what happens. The further away from that big-wig you are, the more disconnected, disenfranchised and disengaged you're likely to be.

And before you say *this doesn't happen in the church*, let us ask: Does anybody else out there know what it's like to follow a legend into the pulpit? Several of us do, but nobody on our team has experienced this more poignantly than Kelly. The first congregation she served as pastor, twenty years ago, had never had a woman in the pulpit before. In fact, they had never even elected a woman to serve on the church council or governing board. But that wasn't her biggest challenge when she arrived full of energy and ideas fresh out of seminary. Like every other pastor who had come before her, she walked right into the shadow of *THE PASTOR WHO SHALL NOT BE NAMED*. Did you hear the big, booming, slightly scary god-voice we just used? We'll call him Pastor Johnson for the sake of this story.

Anyway, Pastor Johnson had been the legend of this country church for over 30 of its 125-year history. For nearly a quarter of their life together, Pastor Johnson had called the shots. He wasn't mean or anything. In fact, all accounts are that he was a much beloved leader in that congregation and in that community. But his word was law. And a benevolent ruler is still a ruler. He was the standard of leadership that every pastor who followed him had to meet. Of course, none of them ever measured up. No pastor since Pastor Johnson retired lasted in that congregation for more than a handful of years. When the one who lasted the longest (eight years) finally left that congregation, he left the ministry altogether.

Even though it had been 30 years since Pastor Johnson hung up his clerical collar and moved to town (yes, 30 years!), and at least a decade since he died, when Kelly arrived, the memory of him was as fresh as ever. Most of the people in that congregation, after all, had been baptized, confirmed and/or married by him. He had buried many of their grandparents and parents, even a few of their children. In the end, Kelly actually loved serving in that little church. And most folks there loved her back. But it wouldn't have been possible if she had had to stay in Pastor Johnson's shadow.

How did she get out from under it? That's a longer story than we have time to tell. But it all started the day, pretty early on, she stood in the pulpit, and with the biggest, goofiest grin she could muster, held her arms out wide to give everybody a good look at her, and dared to say out loud what everyone was already thinking: "Well, as you can all see perfectly well, I'm no Pastor Johnson." (Grin and fade to black.)

Don't be fooled by imitations

To be sure, in most places in North America today there are more humane working conditions and better wages than there were back in the early twentieth century—right around the time that little country congregation was founded and industrialists were changing the way we live and work together. There have been various and valiant attempts to update the old command-and-control framework; make it more relevant in our modern context and take into account the needs of present-day employees and (in the church and non-profit world) volunteers. Some of these efforts have been driven by profit and some of them by principle. But the most popular management programs of recent decades have done virtually nothing to challenge the basic, underlying framework that developed well over a hundred years ago. Why not? Because as long as you're still trying to fill-in-the-blank, you need somebody in charge telling everyone what to do and how to do it. All you can reasonably hope for, if you're stuck in a consumable culture, is to try being a little more humane about it.

If you've ever worked in the corporate world, for example, you might remember Total Quality Management (TQM). TQM is a good example of a recent attempt to humanize a consumable organization. It is a philosophy that basically makes quality—including, in some cases, improving the quality of life for workers and customers—the driving force. There is a humane side to TQM and at its best this approach emphasizes ethics, integrity, trust, training, teamwork, leadership, recognition and communication. But the bottom line goal of TQM is making processes "visible, repeatable, and measurable."[22] In other words, it's all about getting that blank filled in as quickly and efficiently as possible. And its basic approach is management by control.[23] TQM (and its close cousin known as "Six Sigma") have been very popular in the corporate world. Over two-thirds of Fortune 500 companies have implemented a process like this over the past decade.

This approach has been popular in the church, too. About a decade ago, for example, one highly influential church leader and megachurch pastor created an offshoot of TQM that he called Total Quality Ministry.[24] Total Quality Ministry applied TQM processes to the church. Leaders were urged to read and respond quickly and purposefully to the needs and expectations of their customers/constituents; indeed, to anticipate and exceed those expectations and needs. They were exhorted to provide vigorous training for their staff and volunteers in these principles and challenged to measure their results using quantifiable metrics.

Most church growth programs today, in one way or another, echo this approach. And they are widespread. In order to get more bucks in the plate and butts in the pews, congregations and faith-based organizations all across North America have invested countless time and money in writing elaborate strategic plans, setting objective and measurable goals, creating guiding coalitions, grouping their leaders into accountability triads to make sure they do what they're supposed to do, and our personal pet peeve: vision casting. You know, that's where you work really hard trying to get everybody as excited about your vision as you are, even though you never asked them what they might be thinking or dreaming about.

We think that if the original Mr. Ford and his peers could take a reverse commute using our time machine, they would surely approve. Although you might have slapped a little lipstick on it, what you've been using to run your congregation or that faith-based organization of yours is basically the same pet pig Henry Ford had in his shed. You've been using a standard model, 20th century command-and-control, fill-in-the-blank, efficiency-driven model of getting things done. And in most places today—including the congregation where Total Quality Ministry emerged—that has not gone so well.[25]

This is not your daddy's century

There is widespread agreement that in the 21st century, something is different. The way things are being done in our churches and other organizations today might not be very different than they were in the last century—at least, not yet. But the way people think about themselves is changing and has changed.[26] This isn't a generational issue, although it's probably truer for younger folks, by and large. But even older folks don't see themselves quite the same way they used to. Not too many of the oldsters we know, for example, would actually want THE PASTOR WHO SHALL NOT BE NAMED running the show again, no matter what they might tell each other over cookies at the coffee hour after worship.

People see themselves differently than they used to. There are lots of reasons for this, including "increasing globalization, increasing education and affluence."[27] You can blame the internet for this if you want to. What *hasn't* it changed? The blogosphere is jam-packed with people writing about topics that bounce from knitting to politics to fishing to religion to sex. Through online social networking sites (i.e., MySpace, Facebook, Twitter, etc.) people interact as equals across race, gender, class, job title, educational level and ability. The old hierarchies that required addressing your elders—and your "betters"—as "Sir" or "Madam" have all but disappeared. Nobody's in charge of the worldwide web. And everybody likes that just fine.

People today don't want to be told what to do, especially if they haven't been asked for their input. They want more out of the communities and organizations they are part of, and they demand more out of their work. They want their questions, insights and ideas to be taken seriously. They don't like having you waste their time. They believe their intelligence, creativity and passions ought to be put to good use. And honestly, it kind of ticks them off when those things don't happen. This might explain why today's employees are less happy with their jobs than at any point in the past twenty years. Fewer than half of all working Americans, for example, say they are satisfied and that percentage decreases the younger people are. One headline from a major online news outlet reads: "Americans hate their jobs more than ever."[28] It might also explain why at least one major Protestant denomination reports that over one-third of all congregational conflict is due to the pastor's leadership style or personality, or arguments about how decisions should be made.[29] People today will give you everything they've got if they believe they're making a difference. But they aren't satisfied being a part of an organization that sucks the life out of them…even if that organization happens to be a church. If you want to get things done in the 21st century you're going to have to figure out a different way to do it.

People want their work and their lives to matter. They believe they deserve nothing less. And frankly, we think God would agree. In fact, we think in some ways it's fair to say that people are finally catching a glimpse of how God has always intended for us to live and work together.

This really works

Think for a minute about how Jesus interacted with his disciples. Here's an example of the kinds of directions Jesus used to give his crew: "Then Jesus called the twelve together and gave them power and authority over all demons and to cure diseases, and he sent them out to proclaim the kingdom of God and to heal.

He said to them, 'Take nothing for your journey, no staff, nor bag, nor bread, nor money—not even an extra tunic. Whatever house you enter, stay there, and leave from there. Wherever they do not welcome you, as you are leaving that town shake the dust off your feet as a testimony against them." (Luke 9:1-5, *NRSV*) They very quickly discovered that they weren't working for a micromanager. When they got back, they told him how it went. And that was pretty much that.

When this passage gets read by people in our North American context today, it sounds like Jesus is asking the impossible: Leave all of your precious possessions behind. But read his instructions again, in context. Jesus was talking to people who didn't *have* many precious possessions to start with! Jesus wasn't necessarily telling them to leave their stuff behind; what they needed to hear was that it doesn't matter if you have stuff or not. You don't need to wait until you've got a little extra bread or you've saved up enough cash or you've got the right wardrobe. Just go with what you've got and put it to use in a way that makes a difference. This was no fill-in-the-blank ministry. This was no command-and-control operation, either. Jesus didn't create convoluted constitutions constricting their every movement, manuals to read and follow, or clocks to punch. Jesus gave his disciples a job to do. He gave them the authority to do it, and he set them free to use their intelligence, creativity and passion to make it happen in any way that made sense in their context. The whole story of Jesus and his disciples is one of empowerment and freedom. This is especially evident in the story told by the gospel writer called Luke. After Jesus told them they had the "power and authority" to do what he was asking them to do (Luke 9:1) he said:

- *You* do it! (9:13)
- *You* confess! (9:20)
- Take up *your* cross every day (9:24)
- Get ready for my departure (9:31)
- *Your* hands are my hands! (10:16)

Luke continues the story in the Book of Acts, which describes how the message about Jesus gets from Jerusalem to Rome and beyond. The disciples embrace the freedom they had been given and they do whatever they have to do, take their message to whomever will listen—Jews and Gentiles, men and women, slave and free. They cross borders and ignore every wall somebody tries to build in front of them. They experiment with things. They learn from their mistakes. They get the job done without anybody looking over their shoulder or telling them what to do.

In fact, there is very little continuity between how Jesus did things and how his disciples did them after he was gone. Whereas Jesus' ministry was spent mostly among the rural poor, the disciples and early church leaders took their work into mostly urban places like Philippi and Corinth and Rome, and their first converts were often the wealthiest people in town (e.g. Lydia). Those earliest Christians even changed-up the message Jesus preached. Whereas he came proclaiming "the kingdom of God," that's not a phrase his disciples ever used.[30]

The Holy Spirit was at work, empowering, encouraging, challenging and comforting those first Christians. But they were free. They might not have *talked* about the kingdom, but they lived like they knew it was true. This decentralized, bottom-up, permission-giving, empowered organization is not just the best example we could ask for in the quest to live and work in a renewable, life-giving way. It has become arguably one of the most successful operations in the history of humankind. You're reading this book right now because of what those guys did and how they did it. Make the shift.

Looking for God...

...through the biblical story:

Exodus 18:13-27
If you're in a small group, read the passage out loud.

Even three thousand years ago God was pointing us away from a command-and-control way of working together, toward empowerment and decentralization! Jethro told Moses that his real focus should be on teaching people "the statutes and instructions" and making "known to them the way they are to go and the things they are to do" (Ex. 18:20), rather than on telling everyone what to do. Equip them! Empower them! And quit micro-managing. The command-and-control approach was killing Moses—and it wasn't good for the other people, either.

1. How would you have responded to Jethro if you were Moses? Remember, you just parted the Red Sea! You just stood up against the most powerful ruler on earth! Now your father-in-law is giving you advice.

2. When have you received good advice from someone when you needed but didn't necessarily want it? Did you take it? What happened? Why is it important to listen to the wisdom of others even when you think you know what you're doing?

3. Moses gave away power to people all throughout the community— there were "leaders" for every ten people (Ex. 18:21). Essentially, each family was responsible for handling its own issues. As these people spent the next four decades on a journey through the desert, until they finally settled down in the "Promised Land," what difference do you think it made that so many people were empowered to make decisions, handle conflict and take action? How do you think this decentralized, "bottom-up," permission-giving approach contributed to the survival of this community through such uncertain and difficult times?

...through each other:

1. What is your organization's temperature? Identify those places in your organization that don't feel so healthy right now. Would you say that your faith community or organization is facing outward towards its community—or focused more inwardly on its own needs? Why do you say that?

2. In what ways have you experienced the "command-and-control" or "fill in the blank" approach that characterizes a consumable organization at your workplace, your school, another place you volunteer, or somewhere else? Have you ever felt frustrated and even abused by it? In what ways have you experienced these things in your current faith community or organization?

3. What is the fill-in-the-blank phrase that people tend to use in your faith community or organization? What do they *not* have that they keep focusing on? How would the challenges you face look different if you quit trying to fill-in-the-blank and instead, focused on how you can be useful to God right where you are, using what you already have?

4. What does it mean to you to "make the shift" from a consumable to a renewable way of living and working together? Do you agree that this is a critical, even a "moral" issue? Why or why not?

...through your neighbour:

1. In what ways have you seen your co-workers, schoolmates, neighbours, friends you volunteer with, etc., abused by bosses, leaders, teachers, coaches, etc. who use a command-and-control approach? In what ways have you seen people at work, school, etc. "used up" by a consumable system or an organization that is too focused on filling in the blank? If you can find a better, more renewable way to work together in your faith community or organization, what difference do you think it might make to what's happening "out there" in the places people live, work, go to school, volunteer, etc.?

2. Do you know anyone at work, school, another non-profit agency, a group you belong to, who could be an example to you and/or teach you something about how to live and work in a more renewable way (i.e., they bring out the best in people, honour the gifts and passions that people bring, lead in a way that is life-giving to people and to the planet)? Who are they? How do you know them? Give an example that shows why you think they are leading in a renewable way. Contact them over the next two weeks and ask them to go out with you for coffee; find out what motivates them and learn everything you can about how they're doing what they do.

The Back Story

[16] Richard Bradley, "Drew Gilpin Faust and the Incredible Shrinking Harvard," *Boston Magazine*, June 2009.

[17] Nina Munk, "Rich Harvard, Poor Harvard," *Vanity Fair*, August 2009.

[18] Ibid.

[19] Gary Hamel, "Moon Shots for Management," *Harvard Business Review*, Feb. 1, 2009.

[20] Deborah Bruce (project manager), US Congregational Life Survey, 2001, "As part of the U.S. Congregational Life Survey, about 300,000 worshipers in over 2,000 congregations in the United States completed a survey during worship services in April 2001. Worshippers in Australia, England, and New Zealand completed similar surveys. Together, the international effort included about 2 million worshippers and 17,000 congregations across three continents." The data that is reported in this book was collected from worshippers in ELCA congregations; but it is reflective of other Mainline Protestant denominations.

[21] Daniel Pink, A Whole New Mind, (Riverhead Books, NY, 2005, 2006), p. 186.

[22] From an article titled "The Eight Elements of TMQ," by Nayantara Padhi, an HR Executive in an Indian Steel Industry and an expert in TQM, published by iSixSigma, copyright 2000-2008. http://www.isixsigma.com/library/content/c021230a.asp

[23] TQM is a favourite target of postmodern organization theorists, who regard it as a direct descendent of "Taylorism," the management approach developed by Frederick Winslow Taylor in the early twentieth century. Mary Jo Hatch writes in her book, *Organization Theory: Modern, Symbolic, and Postmodern Perspectives* (Oxford University Press, New York, 1997), that "Taylor's system undermined the authority of the workers and their master craftsmen by introducing managerial control and supervision, and by offering differential pay for performance which eroded worker solidarity. These aspects of Scientific Management earned it considerable and lasting ill-repute as being ruinously ignorant of the trust and cooperation between management and workers upon which organizations depend. So much furor was created by Taylor that Scientific Management was the subject of an American Congressional Investigation," p. 31.

[24] Walt Kallestad, *Total Quality Ministry* (Fortress Press, Minneapolis, 1999).

[25] According to the ELCA's trend report, Community Church of Joy (CCOJ) in Glendale, Arizona, experienced steady growth from 1990 to 2001. From 2001-2008, however, the congregation has had a 50% decline in baptized membership, from almost 11,000 to just over 5,000, and a 40% decline in worship attendance. Throughout this decade, the congregation's leadership has tried various approaches to stem the loss and reverse the decline. In 2008, it saw its first increase in worship attendance since 2001, although membership has continued to decline. The senior pastor has described the kind of soul-searching he has done over this past decade. On a ministry-changing sabbatical, after a heart attack, Rev. Kallestad says he came to the realization that they had been very good at "...attracting the crowd, but it wasn't transforming them into empowered disciples. Could it be that our acreage, buildings, and budgets were interfering with the mission instead of accomplishing it? Why weren't we producing empowered disciples? What were we missing?" He and the people of CCOJ are on a new journey these days. "In the old days, staff controlled programming and people came if they wanted to. "Now we have less control," he says, "but the people are accountable to transform their community. Now, that's how we define success: One changed life and one empowered disciple at a time." Kallestad has written about this journey in an article titled "Redefining Success: Moving from Entertainment to Worship," *Theology: News and Notes*, Fuller Theological Seminary, Fall 2008.

[26] Hatch, p. 26.

[27] Thomas Malone, *The Future of Work: How the New Order of Business Will Shape Your Organization, Your Management Style, and Your Life*, (Harvard Business Press, Boston, 2006), p. 26.

[28] These 2007 survey results, reported by MSNBC.com, are from The Conference Board, a market information company that also puts out the Consumer Confidence Index and the Leading Economic Indicators. http://www.msnbc.msn.com/id/17348695/

[29] 2000 Survey of United Church of Christ Congregations, http://fact.hartsem.edu/denom/UCCreport.pdf

[30] Thanks to Professor Ed Krentz for these insights, shared during a course on Evangelism in the New Testament at the Lutheran School of Theology at Chicago in the summer of 2001.

4

A New Way of Being

"Stand firm, therefore, and do not submit again to a yoke of slavery." — Galatians 5:1b

The organizations that can't or won't make the shift from a consumable to a renewable way of living and working together will find themselves becoming increasingly toxic; as poisonous to people as they are to the planet. They will not survive the emerging future. This goes for faith communities and faith-based organizations, too. For people of faith however, making this shift from a consumable to a renewable way of living and working ought to be a no-brainer. Not only do we have the example of Jesus to follow as we live and work together, we have the freedom to actually do it. We know that God is on a loving mission to reconcile all creation and set people free.

This mission comes *to* you, through Jesus Christ, and it comes *through* you to the world. Jesus has set you free to:

- **Be who you are;**
- **See what you have;**
- **Do what matters.**

Pretty simple, eh? Well, don't be fooled. Simple is not the same thing as easy. Maybe you've seen the little book called *101 Things You Should Know How to Do*. The introduction promises that "You'll love this book. It's an absolutely essential collection of clear and straightforward advice—everything you need to start coping with the miscellany of modern life."[31] And we do, in fact, love it.

Each chapter describes how to do something almost everybody wishes at some point they knew how to do. The chapters cover such things as how to: play poker, speed-read, read music, take a power-nap, get served in a crowded bar and how to unclog a sink. The descriptions in each chapter are as clear and uncomplicated as they could possibly be. The whole book is only 252 pages long. That means each chapter gets about two pages and about half the pages have some kind of simple drawing or illustration. At the end of each chapter you feel like you really *could* perform CPR, swim or dance the waltz. But actually being able to glide around the dance floor with a competent partner is another thing entirely. Have you seen the popular reality TV show, *Dancing With The Stars?* We have.

Likewise, making the shift from a consumable approach to a renewable one is simple. But that doesn't mean it's easy. You're most likely going to need help. Especially in turbulent times, people are tempted to go back to the old, "tried-and-true" ways of doing things; experimentation seems too risky; leaders

" Be who you are "

feel like they have to "take charge."[32] You may be feeling that way right now. Stand firm and refuse to let anything put you back into bondage. Do everything you can to avoid getting sucked back into the fill-in-the-blank game. If you're a leader, resist with all your might the urge to return to the old command-and-control approach. There is no shortcut to renewability. The Renewable Organization is a system that can help you get there.

" See what you have "

The processes and practices within this system train you to *be who you are and see what you have for the sake of doing what matters to God.* They can help your organization become more playful, purposeful, fruitful, adaptable and resilient. They will make it possible for you to embrace the emerging future by replacing that old consumable and centralized approach to life and work with a more organic, sustainable and decentralized way of being and doing.

The system is powered by a set of seven Renewable Practices. These practices are the antidote to the command-and-control way of living and working together that characterizes a consumable organization. They can help you create a culture that allows and encourages people to bring their *whole* selves—every ounce of creativity, intelligence and passion they have within them—to your common work.

Research has shown that when people are wholly engaged they get more done and they do what matters. We have found that, when used by leaders, these practices not only engage people, they can give you and the people you work with the freedom to really *be who you are*. **Be who you are** is the first of three principles at the heart of a Renewable Organization.

> ❝ *Do what matters* ❞

The Renewable Practices include:

- *Asking Purposeful Questions*
- *Using Participative Processes*
- *Working Playfully*
- *Taking Place Seriously*
- *Being Reproductive*
- *Seeing Possibilities*
- *Igniting Passion*

These practices look simple, but they are not easy. Practice them every day, in every single situation and they will help you tap into and transform that treasure of extraordinary power that dwells within your clay jar.

 Asking Purposeful Questions

The first practice is **Asking Purposeful Questions**, and it's your first clue that a renewable way of living and working together is probably unlike anything you've experienced before.

It used to be that people expected leaders to have all the answers. The whole command-and-control structure is built on the idea that the person in charge knows what the rest of us should be thinking, saying and doing. This has been as true in the church as anywhere. Just look at the way pastors are being trained. In most seminary classrooms you'll still find rows of men and women sitting with their attention focused on the expert behind the lectern at the front, soaking up all the knowledge and wisdom they can, so that they can fan out into congregations across the country where they will be the ones standing at the front of the room doling out knowledge and wisdom. Naturally, these pastors-to-be are tested and examined and poked and prodded before they're turned loose. In this system, it's imperative to know that the leaders know all the answers.

Except no one believes they do. In the church today (as in any other kind of organization), people may still expect their leaders to *act* like they have all the answers. But deep down they know better. People today know that enormous and uncontrollable changes are happening all around them (and even inside of them). They know there are no pat answers and no easy solutions. They know it's going to take all of us working together to enter the emerging future. They know that answers are the last thing they need from their leaders. What they really need is help wrestling with the big questions, the "Why?" questions; the questions of meaning and purpose.

Every Tuesday morning the team here at ARE spends an hour on the phone together in "centering time." One morning we reflected on the TED (Technology, Entertainment, Design) presentation by Jacek Ukto, a young Polish-born designer who is being credited with turning around the newspaper business in multiple western and eastern European nations. How did he do it? He said the key has been asking purposeful questions: Why are we here? What are we trying to accomplish? What is the point?[33]

People who are courageous and smart enough to spend time really wrestling with these questions together find that they come out so committed to their common purpose that they are willing to do whatever it takes and change whatever needs changing in order to achieve it. They don't get stuck on doing things "the way we've always done them." They don't argue about things that don't matter. Their traditions, rituals, rules, etc. take a back seat to their common goals. They can adapt to any new situation. They lean into the future. People today are longing for a sense of meaning and purpose. Your job as a leader is to help people ask the purposeful questions; the questions of meaning in your common work. This is true no matter what kind of organization you are leading. Studies have shown that "letting spirituality into the workplace [doesn't] distract organizations from their

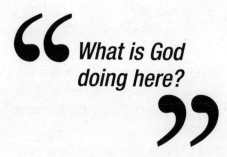

What is God doing here?

goals. It often help[s] them reach those goals."[34]

For church leaders, of course, the purposeful questions are always the *God* questions: What is God doing here? What is making God smile? What is breaking God's heart? What do we need to stop doing so that we can be more useful to God? What do we need to start doing? Where does God want us to focus our resources that will really make a difference?

Asking the right questions doesn't come naturally or easily to most people though. Even Jesus' followers, in the last moments they had with him, wanted to know, *But when are you going to restore Israel?! When are you going to kick out the Romans?! When are you going to fix our problems?!* One of the final things Jesus said to them was, *Guys! You're not asking the right questions!* (Acts 1:6-7).

It takes discipline. It takes practice. Above all, it takes refusing to play the role of know-it-all. Let's be honest, in this complex and changing context, you *don't* know it all. And whether they'll dare to say it to your face or not, everybody knows it. The most important thing you can bring to every table, every conversation and every room is a determination to help people move "beyond themselves"[35] to serve something larger than themselves. Your job is to invite them, whenever you can and in whatever it is you're doing, deeper into God's mission to reconcile the whole creation and set people free.

 ## Using Participative Processes

The second practice that can help you tap into the treasure of extraordinary power that dwells within the people you've been called to work with and serve beside is ***Using Participative Processes***.

Working collaboratively and getting others involved, especially at the highest levels of decision making, is just as foreign to most leaders as bringing questions (rather than answers) to the table. Most leaders today simply haven't been trained in using participative processes. Many of them are skeptical that it can even work. The old command-and-control model says the leader needs to be "The Decider." But that's how we end up having good ideas, good questions and good people flattened by top-down organizations. It's bad enough if people come to work for you because you pay them. But it is deadly if the people who work in your organization or belong to your community are mostly volunteers.

Thomas Malone, who teaches management at the MIT Sloan School of Management and regularly consults with businesses across the country, dares to make people name the damage they do to each other in their life together. He has said, "When I give talks about new organizations, I often take a little poll to see how well the audience thinks today's companies take advantage of people's abilities. I ask them this question: What percentage of the intelligence and creativity of the people in your own organization do you think your organization actually uses?" He says the average answer is from 30 to 40 percent.[36]

Using Malone's question, we have been taking a similar survey into the organizations we work with. What's different about our survey is that we are usually asking the leaders of these organizations. Our audience typically includes committee chairs, team leaders, elected board members, senior staff, pastors, rostered leaders and judicatory executives. The results of our informal polling have been nearly identical to the ones Malone reports from his surveys.

If leaders say that only 30 to 40 percent of their passions, intelligence, gifts and abilities are getting tapped by the organizations they care about, we can only imagine what the average member or volunteer in these organizations would say.

Malone concludes: "…the results [of this informal polling] highlight a strong feeling most of us share: Organizations today come nowhere close to realizing and taking advantage of people's true potential."[37] Instead of flattening people, we need to be flattening the organizational structures of our faith communities and faith-based organizations.

You may already be discovering that in this fast-paced and quickly changing context you really do need everybody at the table. The newest person in the room often has the best input because she is seeing everything with new eyes. The guys who have spent their years on the margins because they're 'different' or because they're 'just' support staff, usually have valuable insights that could make things better for everybody. The biblical story is full of one example after another of how God was at work in and through the most unlikely person, changing everything for good. Why would you think you can do it all on your own? Remember—even Jesus didn't work alone.

The job of a leader in a Renewable Organization is to facilitate the kinds of conversations that lead to good ideas and the best decisions, rather than feeling like it's her responsibility (or right!) to make all the decisions herself, and to create a culture that not only allows everyone to bring what they have to offer but expects them to.

Resist the urge to "take charge" in a way that shuts people down and shuts them up. "A tried and true maxim of [the] field of organizational behavior is that 'people support what they create.'"[38] Lead by getting people around the table to bring their energy, intelligence and enthusiasm to every problem and every project. Ask people what they think. Listen to them. Involve them. Whenever possible, let the people decide.

Margaret Wheatley is an organization theorist who has worked with organizations of all types and sizes across the globe. With amazement and awe she describes what she has seen happen when people come together from all parts of an organization to create shared visions and plans. Wheatley asks: "Why would we stay locked in our belief that there is one right way to do something, or one correct interpretation to a situation, when the universe demands diversity and thrives on a plurality of meaning? Why would we avoid participation and worry only about its risks, when we need more and more eyes to be wise? Why would we resist the powerful visions and futures that emerge when we come together to co-create the world?" Why, indeed?

 ## Working Playfully

The third Renewable Practice, **Working Playfully**, is going to be a challenge for many church folk to get their heads around, but play is being taken very seriously in the business world today. The mission statement of Southwest Airlines, one of the few carriers that seems to be making it these days (at least for the moment), says "People rarely succeed at anything unless they are having fun doing it." And more than fifty European companies, including Nokia, Alcatel and others, are using "Serious Play," a technique that uses Lego® building blocks to unleash the creativity of their employees.[39] But in the church we're not so sure.

Play belongs in the Sunday school room or at camp, but not in our very serious business meetings, and certainly not in worship. A long history which values a strong Protestant work ethic has served to create a filter through which work and fun are seen as mutually exclusive. You work first and when your work is done you play. Somehow we seem to have missed the fact that our Saviour came in the form of a child and nobody is better at playing than children.

It's time to ask for the crayons back.[40]

Wheatley, who has grown sick and tired to death of organizational charts and schedules and plans, argues that the modern approach to life and work has been deeply influenced by a kind of Newtonian thinking that encouraged and allowed people to treat organizations like they were machines. Remember Newton's scientific theories from your high school science class? For example, "A body persists its state of rest or of uniform motion unless acted upon by an external unbalanced force." Newton's "laws" convinced us all that eventually we could figure everything out and, therefore, control it. Well, we can't. And we won't.

The emerging world of quantum science is "weird and fascinating," revealing things at a subatomic level that Newton's laws just can't explain; it "challenges so many of our basic assumptions, including our understanding of relationships, connectedness, prediction, and control."[41] These scientific discoveries are impacting the way people think about everything. The universe isn't a machine and neither is the organization you care about. It is organic and, as such, subject to change and chaos, possessing the capacity to adapt and to grow. You cannot successfully control it. But you can co-create within it. You can stay aware of what is happening and respond in ways that are smart and brave. You can work together, experimenting with new ways of doing things. You can commit yourself to learning from each other, from your environment, from your mistakes. And only people who know how to play can do these things.

In a renewable organization, work and play go hand in hand. We're not saying that it has to be fun all the time. But if it is never fun, you are not doing the right thing or at least may not be doing it the right way. Your best work is no laughing matter, but it just might be laughter that helps you do your best work. Working playfully makes work more enjoyable, it creates a safe place for people to be creative and try new things, and it helps build trust. Laughter is the sign of a healthy, adaptable and resilient organization—churches, too.[42]

When our team goes in to work with a faith community or a faith-based group to help them revision or retool for God's mission, we pray a lot. We get people diving into the biblical story. We help them meet their neighbours and find out what other people across their organization are thinking. But maybe the most important thing we do is to help them play together. We take toys with us—paper and crayons, stuff to build with, games that get people moving and laughing together. We believe the best way into the emerging future is to play your way there.

Taking Place Seriously

Taking Place Seriously is the fourth practice and it ought to be natural for people who believe in an incarnate God who took on our flesh and dwelled among us. If Jesus took our context seriously enough to enter it—literally—shouldn't we want to engage it too?

We have a hard time understanding the fear, suspicion and outright disdain that so many Christians have for the world outside the doors of their church building. We remember hearing, for example, about how the Anglican Archbishop of Wales got into a wee bit of hot water a few years back. Seems he agreed to participate in an open debate about the question, "Is Religion Bad?" The problem was the debate was being held in a bar. People were horrified and offended. Not the people in the bar, of course (although some of them might have been a little freaked out to see an Archbishop in a bar), but people in the church (who of course never go to the bar).[43]

The problem with hiding from "the world" is that *God is on the loose out there.* Taking place seriously is about way more than just being contextual, although that is certainly important. It's a good thing to learn how to speak the language of people in your context, to discover what matters to them, to fall in love with their food and their customs, to learn *from* them and learn how to share what matters to you in a way that makes sense to them. But taking place seriously is more than all that. It's about being on the lookout for God in your midst, so that you can ride the momentum that God is already creating in and through people where you live, work, serve, learn and play.

We find it fascinating that social innovators—people who work for transformative social change, especially on behalf of vulnerable populations—have discovered that the power they need to get things done usually lies outside of themselves. All they have to do is pay attention so they don't miss it when it comes and then ride it as best they can. "In complexity science this is called emergence, a term used to describe things that are unpredictable, which seem to result from the interactions between elements, and are outside of any one agent's control."[44] Social innovators know intuitively that if they are open to it, the power they need to effect change will eventually find them. People of faith know that power belongs to God.

When you take place seriously, you keep your eyes open for what God is up to in your midst. You're not trying to command or control people; you see their assets, gifts and passions and you want to unleash them for the sake of making a difference in the world. You see the amazing things God is already doing in and through people inside and outside of your organization. You recognize the unique opportunities you have to make a difference in the community you have been called to serve. There is power out there. Pay attention.

 Being Reproductive

One of the characteristics of a consumable approach to ministry is the preponderance of programs offered by congregations eager to snag new members. *If you have a need we'll meet it*, is the mantra of this kind of church. Congregations see themselves as service-providers. Pastors are expected to be caretakers, hand holders and CEOs. The downside of this approach is easy to measure: congregational members burned out by the demand to provide one program after another, pastors exhausted by carrying the burdens of so many needy people. And a shopper's mentality infecting everyone concerned; *if this congregation doesn't meet my needs, I'll find one that does.*

Knowing that competition is fierce, congregations are under increasing pressure to deliver goods and services more quickly and efficiently than the church down the street. The same goes for every faith-based organization out there. A command-and-control approach seems like the only way to get things done. But this way of working is wrong in almost every way.

The church of our emerging future will serve neighbour and care for the planet, but it will not derive its sense of purpose from hand holding. That goes for other faith-based organizations as well. ***Being Reproductive*** is the fifth practice and it is about recognizing that there is a treasure of extraordinary power within the people God has created. Whatever your particular ministry happens to be, it is your call to help people recognize that power in themselves, so they can put it into action in a way that makes a real difference in the world. You have been called to reproduce disciples, not dependents; to raise up co-workers in the kingdom of God.

Thomas Malone has argued that one of the keys to transforming the old command-and-control approach is to think about your job as a leader as "cultivation" rather than control. The way to talk about being reproductive is to ask yourself how do you cultivate people? He offers a few suggestions: First, harness their natural tendencies. Instead of trying to get people to love what you love and do what you do, find out what they are passionate about and good at. Help them put those passions and gifts to good use. Second, let a thousand flowers bloom. Instead of telling people what to do, encourage them to experiment. When something works, resource it. If it doesn't work, let it die. Debrief what happened and help people learn from what they do. In this way you'll give them opportunities to grow and you'll create a culture of mass experimentation. Third, encourage cross-fertilization. In other words, create opportunities for people to learn from each other and not just from you. Reproducing disciples is about raising up co-workers; it isn't about creating a bunch of "mini-mes." For example, re-imagine when, where and how you conduct meetings; put people who wouldn't usually work together in the same room; give people a chance to dream, play, pray and plan together. Fourth, embrace opportunities to improvise. If you're cultivating leaders, there will be a lot of change; there will be unexpected problems, and you won't be able to plan everything ahead of time. This isn't something to be endured, if you're serious about being reproductive. You'll be thankful every time you get to respond to an unexpected opportunity.[45]

Remember that you are cloning yourself whether you know it or not. Be intentional about the DNA you're passing along. Start looking at every single thing you do in ministry as being about making disciples—yes, even pastoral care—even (at the risk of starting a riot) worship; identify your "replacement" and spend time mentoring him/her; challenge five people a year, face to face, to grow in their financial giving. (Of course, that means your own house has to be in order. Only leaders who *are* disciples can reproduce them.) Give away power; share leadership; cultivate people.

 ## Seeing Possibilities

Researchers in the growing field of social innovation have discovered that "fierce conviction is required to sustain innovation through various internal and external struggles, and to be an agent for change requires bold thinking and grand vision. Complexity theory shows that great changes can emerge from small actions, that the possible, even the 'impossible,' can happen. That's the part about keeping your head in the stars. But what about keeping your feet on the ground? How do social innovators do that? They face reality." [46]

The sixth practice, **Seeing Possibilities**, means daring to see—to really see—the good, the bad and the ugly. This is what Jesus did when he warned his disciples that their great adventure was going to end up at the cross (Mark 8:31-33). Peter wasn't too happy about this, of course. Jesus told him he sounded a little like Satan. For Jesus—like every change-agent that has come after him—"Hell is not failing; hell is delusion. Hell is kidding yourself about what's going on..." [47] Seeing possibilities is about staying "fiercely visionary and hopeful even while determinedly grounding [your] actions in the cold heaven of daily reality testing." [48]

Facing reality isn't something church leaders have been very good at. For example, we have met with church leaders who dreamed of having a growing church. What they envisioned was a Sunday school full of little blond-haired kids; a flock of stay-at-home moms who could run all the programs and bake all the cookies; and a stable full of handsome dads (all wearing ties of course), driving the whole family to church each Sunday morning. When we asked these church leaders to go out and actually meet their neighbours, they discovered that they had been trying to do ministry with their heads in the sand. Out on their street they heard a dozen different languages and listened to a hundred unique narratives—and there wasn't a single blond kid in sight. At first, they were stunned because their dream no longer seemed possible to fulfill. But, in fact, all kinds of new ministries become possible when you are willing to face reality.

When you are captive to how things used to be or to foolish ambitions of what you think should be you're more inclined to function in a command-and-control way, killing yourself and each other as you claw your way through a living hell.

Seeing possibilities, on the other hand, is about trusting God to do miracles in and through you as you work with what you've got, within the context in which you've been placed. It's about engaging the present and trusting in the future. It's about keeping your feet on the ground and your head in the stars. Seeing possibilities sets you free to be who you really are.

Igniting Passion

Being in last place does not mean this seventh practice, **Igniting Passion**, is least important. In fact, without it, your effort to move from a consumable approach to a renewable one will inevitably fail.

One of the characteristics of a renewable approach is transforming that old command-and-control structure you've inherited into a more collaborative, decentralized way of living and working together. But your organization was centralized for a reason. That traditional hierarchy held

> **Do people know how to listen and speak to each other?**

everything and everybody together. What holds everything together when you flatten the hierarchy and expect everybody to participate in the creation of new things, giving your power away in the process? What prevents the whole project from devolving into utter and destructive chaos?—Relationships. Relationships become more important than ever in a decentralized system.[49] In a system that levels the playing field and takes everyone's gifts and passions into consideration, people have to love each other. You, as the leader, have to love people. And you all have to share a passion for your common work.

Wheatley says that when she used to consult with a firm, she would look at its tasks, functions, span of control and hierarchies. Now, instead, she looks at its capacity for "healthy relationships." Do people know how to listen and speak to each other? To work well with diverse members? Do people have free access to one another throughout the organization? Are they trusted with open information? Do organizational values bring them together or keep them apart? Can people speak truthfully to one another? In organizations where leaders disregard people and the gifts they bring, there is a high level of energy but it's all negative. But when people have healthy relationships, the energy is positive. In other words, power is created by relationships. And what is more powerful in a relationship than love?[50]

That message is what your faith community needs from you, maybe more than any other. They need to know that you believe that no matter what the future holds, God is there, because God loves you and the world you have been called to serve. People need to know that you believe this deeply enough to suffer for it. The Christian story says that's what Jesus did when he willingly suffered and died for the sake of a new future for

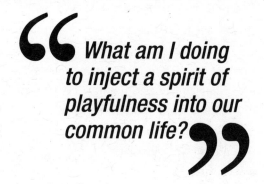

What am I doing to inject a spirit of playfulness into our common life?

humankind. When Christians remember the Passion of Our Lord during Holy Week, they are remembering his suffering. In fact, in Latin, these two words are related: Passion —Suffering.

What are you so committed to that you are willing to endure a little pain to make happen? What dream are you passionate enough about that you're willing to give everything you've got to make it so? What cause are you willing to die for? Tell that story. Share that dream. Listen to the stories and the dreams of those you're working with and serving beside. Let their passion fan the flames of your own. Ignite your passion in others. Let the passion that emerges around your common purpose drive everything you do. And, above all else, love.

* For more on The Renewable Practices see the seven booklets that make up *The Renewable Practices Series.*

Some key questions

The seven Renewable Practices are the antidote to the command-and-control way of leading that characterizes consumable organizations. They power a renewable organization by tapping into and unleashing the treasure of extraordinary power that dwells within your clay jars. If at least one of these seven practices doesn't challenge you, you're not paying attention.

Making the shift from a consumable to a renewable approach in the faith community or organization you care about begins when you decide to stop pretending you can muster up enough enthusiasm, evidence or incentives to get people to go where you want them to go. You must be ready to serve, to give, to listen, to play, to fail and to learn. You need to let yourself love the people you are privileged to live with and work beside. And in moments of frustration, don't look around for someone to blame. Instead, ask yourself:

What am I doing to keep myself, and others I'm working with, focused on our common purpose?

What am I doing to involve people at every level of this organization in the work of dreaming, planning and taking action?

When was the last time I asked people what they were thinking?

Who do I need to invite into this conversation?

Whose voice needs to be heard because it is brand new and/or has been silenced for too long?

What am I doing to inject a spirit of playfulness into our common life?

In what ways am I letting people know it's okay to try new things, take risks and even make mistakes? How am I modeling this in my own work and life?

When was the last time I stopped (and asked others to stop) and listen for what God is saying to us?

When was the last time I reminded us all to ask the most important question: "What is God doing here...and how can we help?"

For most leaders in the church today, exploring these purposeful questions will mean a whole new way of being.

Looking for God

...through the biblical story:

Mark 10:13-16
If you are in a small group, read the passage out loud.

Elsewhere in the story Jesus uses playful images and stories to describe the kingdom of heaven as a "right here – right now" kind of place where the prodigal son is welcomed home, one found sheep is reason for rejoicing, the king's table has a place for people who dress in rags, and the mustard seed becomes a mighty tree. No wonder he says you have to be like a child to believe or receive this! Possibly, you have heard or read this story a thousand times. This time, read it like Jesus actually meant these words. Read them like he is actually talking to you and your faith community/organization.

1. What are the child-like qualities that are necessary to receive the gifts that God wants to give you? What kinds of things did you love to do as a child? What were your favourite games or toys? Why? What child-like qualities have you lost but need to regain? How can you cultivate those in yourself?

2. If you had more child-like qualities, what would be different about the way you live, work, serve and lead? What would be different about your faith community or organization if you all had those child-like qualities?

...through each other:

1. What percentage of your creativity, passion, energy and intelligence is your faith community or organization putting to good use? What would happen if you, and the people you work with and serve beside, were able to bring even 50% of your gifts and talents to your common work? How about 100%?! What would it feel like to be a part of that community/organization? What could be accomplished? Paint a picture with words of what it would be like.

2. When you are in leadership, how hard is it for you to relinquish control? Name one action that you can take in the next week to help build an environment where the people you work with or serve beside, have more freedom to create, decide, do, etc. What would you do with your time if you didn't have to look over anybody's shoulder or tell them what to do?

3. Which one of the seven Renewable Practices are you the most excited about? Which one do you find the most challenging? Which one do you think is the most important? Which one do you think your faith community or organization needs from you the most, right now? Why? Where can you start teaching these practices to your leaders right now? Where can you start using them right now? Who would be open to learning more about them with you?

4. How healthy are the relationships in your faith community or organization? Do people know how to listen and speak to each other? To work well with diverse members? Do people have free access to one another throughout the organization? Are they trusted with open information? Do organizational values bring them together or keep them apart? Can people speak truthfully to one another? Do you love one another? How can you cultivate these things more intentionally?

5. What would happen if, in every single situation (in your own everyday life and in your life together), you were asking this purposeful question: *What in the world is God up to...and how can I/we help?*

...through your neighbour:

1. Where is the most surprising place you have seen God at work lately "out there" where you live, work, play, learn or serve? What happened? Tell the story. Over the next two weeks, create opportunities for other people in your faith community or organization to tell their stories, too.

2. When did you first fall in love with your neighbourhood/community? What do you love about it now? (If you can't answer these questions, what are you going to do about it?)

The Back Story

[31] Michael Powell, *101 Things You Should Know How To Do*, (Metro Books & Gusto Company AS 2005).

[32] Tom Malone, writing in *The Future of Work* (Harvard Business School Press, 2004), observes that in troubled times, "humans are often tempted to retreat. We look to powerful centralized leaders to save and protect us. We want to go back to the way things used to be…" But he says "the solution to our problems lies not in going back to the old ways, but in going forward to the new ones; not in looking to authority figures to protect us, but in figuring out for ourselves new things to try…" There are no easy answers. But "when future generations look back…they will likely realize that the huge, centralized, hierarchical corporations of the twentieth century were not the pinnacle of business organization." They were an aberration. The future—like the past—is what Malone calls "decentralization."

[33] "Jacek Ukto designs to save newspapers," TED: Ideas Worth Spreading, Posted online March 2009 at http://www.ted.com/index.php/talks/jacek_utko_asks_can_design_save_the_newspaper.html.

[34] Daniel Pink, writing in *A Whole New Mind* (Riverhead Books, NY, 2005, 2006), p. 224. Pink cites several studies showing the importance of "meaning" in the workplace, including this one by Ian Mitroff, a professor at the University of Southern California's Marshall School of Business, and Elizabeth Denton—they published their results in a report called "A Spiritual Audit of Corporate America." Their research found that "companies that acknowledged spiritual values and aligned them with company goals outperformed those that did not."

[35] Dr. Martin Seligman, a professor at the University of Pennsylvania who became head of the American Psychological Association in 1998, has described the highest form of happiness this way: "…the pursuit of meaning…knowing what your strengths are and deploying them in the service of something larger than you are."—Daniel Pink, p. 226.

[36] Malone, p. 153.

[37] Ibid, p.153.

[38] Margaret Wheatley, *Leadership and the New Science*, (Berrett-Koehler Publishers, Inc.), p. 68. Wheatley argues that "this is a world of process, the process of connecting, where 'things' come into temporary existence because of relationship. Whereas "traditional organization charts are filled with lines connecting well-bounded boxes." What's "critical is the availability of places for the exchange of energy." Creating those places, Wheatley says, is the proper role of leadership today.

[39] Pink, pp. 187-188.

[40] Hugh MacLeod, *Ignore Everybody (And 39 Other Keys To Creativity)*, (Portfolio-Penguin Group, 2009), p. 26-28.

[41] Wheatley, pp. 31-33.

[42] Pink includes "play" as one of the "six senses" people will need to succeed in this new "Conceptual Age." Laughter, he says, is the outcome of play and it is a sign of vital relationships—one of the keys to "joyfulness, which in turn can lead to greater creativity, productivity, and collaboration," p. 204.

[43] "Church leader quizzed by clubbers," BBC, August 20, 2007.

[44] Frances Westley, Brenda Zimmerman, and Michael Quinn Patton, *Getting To Maybe: How The World is Changed*, (Random House Canada, 2006), p. 128.

[45] Malone, pp. 155-160.

[46] Westley, et al, p. 168.

[47] Westley, et al, p. 176.

[48] Ibid.

[49] This is the perspective of symbolic-interpretivists and postmodernists in the field of organization theory who see social structure, which is primarily about human relationships, and organizational culture—including shared meaning, understanding, values, belief systems, knowledge, and symbols—as being the key to integration (i.e., holding everything together) in increasingly decentralized organizations. cf. Mary Jo Hatch, *Organization Theory: Modern, Symbolic, and Postmodern Perspectives*, (Oxford, 1997), chapters 6-7. We share this view.

[50] Wheatley, p. 40.

5

A New Way of Seeing

"Then Jesus laid his hands on [the blind man's] eyes again; and he looked intently and his sight was restored, and he saw everything clearly." — Mark 8:25

In organizations of every type and every size, leaders are beginning to recognize that because people think about themselves differently, they need to do things differently, too. Usually, you can tell you've stepped into an organization like this within the first few minutes.

In our neighbourhood, for example, there are two large grocery stores. In the store we avoid, the employees rarely smile. No one ever has an answer to your question. In fact, it's hard to find anyone to even ask a question of; the workers spend more time off in the corner yakking it up and gossiping with each other than they do out on the floor helping customers. The place is poorly lit and more than a little dingy. Don't bother asking for double bags if you have a heavy load or anything else that might sound like extra work; we've actually heard employees swearing under their breath at a customer who had the audacity to do so. We've also heard them swearing under their breath about their boss. Their disdain for their employer is palpable; they seem miserable just being there.

In the store we love, on the other hand, the employees go out of their way to ask if you need help finding whatever it is you're looking for. They are knowledgeable, friendly and ever-present. The place is bright and clean. No request is too outrageous. Workers clearly love what they do and the people they do it with. They are proud of their store. They're ready to tell you all the reasons you should come work for their company. They can describe the suggestions they've made and the changes they've instituted to make the place better. When a new employee is hired by the manager, the people in that department all get to vote, at the end of her thirty-day trial period, on whether or not to add her permanently to the team. And since they get a monthly bonus based on how their department performs, the employees know their voice and their vote really matter.[51]

The folks at the Whole Foods grocery store in our neighbourhood are passionate about what they do and they do it with a deep sense of purpose. They know they are respected, valued and important. They feel like what they do and the way they do it matters. They know they are part of an organization that is making a difference in their community and in the world. Our hunch is that you can walk into any store that is a part of this organization, anywhere in the country, and find exactly the same thing.

Things really can be different. In some places, they already are. It is possible to make the shift from a consumable to a renewable way of living and working together. It is possible to become a renewable church. It begins with transforming the old command-and-control way of getting things done, so that people can be set free to be who they really are; to bring their whole selves—all of their passion, creativity and energy to your common work. And it means learning to see what you have. **Seeing what you have** is the second principle that is at the core of a Renewable Organization. To help you do that we have developed the simple but radical PAWN Process to help you see things in a new way. Just as the seven Renewable Practices provide an antidote to a command-and-control way of doing things, the PAWN Process can be just the antidote you need to the fill-in-the-blank approach that also characterizes a consumable church.

Seeing things in a new way

Somewhere in the Upper Midwest USA, if it's summer, there is a turtle race going on. In one small town that bills itself as the turtle-racing capital of the world, the turtle-racing truck pulls in about mid-morning. The track gets unloaded and assembled right in the middle of Main Street, where a giant yellow ring has been painted with the word "Start" in the centre of it. The barrels, full of ready to race turtles, are rolled into place. The donut-hole stand is erected. The coffee is brewed. And the people come.

Some of the most avid turtle racers bring their own home grown turtle, fresh out of the backyard pond. They're always the odds-on favourites once the races begin. But others, usually the visitors who are camped out on the edge of town or have rented a room at a nearby lodge, rent a turtle for the day. They get to pick their own green racer out of the barrel. And the heat is on.

Turtle-racing (and the donut-hole eating that goes along with it) is a favourite family activity in these northern exposure towns. It always draws a crowd. And the crowd always goes away happy, having gotten their fill of homemade cotton candy and snow cones, wearing a brand new turtle-racing T-shirt and (if they're just brave and/or silly enough) a turtle green foam hat in the shape of their favourite racer. But what impresses us isn't the wholesome picture these turtle races paint of small-town Americana (or the extent to which people in small towns will go to be entertained). What we're fascinated by is this question: Who thought this up? We'd like to meet that guy.

Imagine the day he sat down to tell his family that he was going to start a turtle-racing business. Did they look at him like he was nuts? Did they ask him to repeat himself, thinking maybe they misunderstood what he was saying? Did they laugh at him? Did they congratulate him on his ingenuity? Did they slap their foreheads, stunned at the obviousness of it all, and say to themselves, "Why didn't we think of that?" Did they offer to help?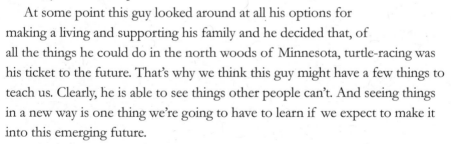

At some point this guy looked around at all his options for making a living and supporting his family and he decided that, of all the things he could do in the north woods of Minnesota, turtle-racing was his ticket to the future. That's why we think this guy might have a few things to teach us. Clearly, he is able to see things other people can't. And seeing things in a new way is one thing we're going to have to learn if we expect to make it into this emerging future.

The 21st century will require no less of an entrepreneurial spirit from church leaders (and everybody else, for that matter) than the 1st century did. Picture Paul, showing up in a new town, his tent-making tools tucked into his knapsack, heading right for the marketplace to set up shop or to meet someone in whose shop he could work. That's how he met Aquilla and Priscilla (Acts 18:1-18). It's how he made a living. It was the easiest way for him to meet new people, to make friends. Some of these friends, like Lydia, opened their homes to host the gathering of new believers who inevitably emerged whenever Paul was around (Acts 16:11-15). Others became Paul's co-workers and travelling companions (Acts 13:1-2). Still others, no doubt the wealthier merchants Paul met at the town square, helped fund his journeys. Paul didn't try to be something he wasn't. As far as we know, for example, the apostle never did learn how to fish.

Paul had, however, learned the secret of being who you are and seeing what you have for the sake of doing what matters. He leveraged his tent-making ability to make a difference in the lives of the people he met. And these people had an impact on him, too. It was in the meeting, the mutual befriending, the living and working together that Paul's whole theological framework began to come undone. His eyes were opened, no less dramatically than they were on that Damascus Road (Acts 9), to a new understanding of what God is up to in this world; to the truth that God is on a mission to reconcile the *whole* creation and set *all* people free; to the really and truly Good News that, in Christ, there is no distinction between one kind of person and another. God calls each one of us (Jew and Gentile alike), loves us and gives each of us work to do that shapes our lives and fills it with meaning and purpose (Galatians 3:27-29).

Paul, the tent-maker changed the world and the world changed him. The energy created by this Spirit-filled dynamic propelled that early church into its emerging future. We're not exactly sure how it happened, but somewhere between then and now 'church leadership' became code language for maintaining institutions, passing on traditions and ensuring good order. That needs to stop.

We realize that, if you're a church leader, you may be under a little (or a lot of) pressure right now to behave yourself—use the proper hymnal, fill out the proper forms, write your sermon (yes, *write* it, pastor; no ad-libbing, no speaking from the heart allowed) using the proper outline format. One newly-minted pastor we know spent a whole summer worrying about the proper wardrobe to take with her into a first call. The church isn't the only institution to impose an acceptable way of thinking, being and doing onto its participants—just ask anyone who has spent time in the corporate world. But the church is awfully good at it. We know. We've been there.

Some of our teammates are better at behaving than others, but every single one of us knows what it's like to be a part of a system that seems hell-bent on crushing any bit of creativity, ingenuity or initiative God might have given you. A few of us know what it's like to be marginalized and even pushed out when who we are, how we see things, and what we bring to the table become too much for the system to bear. We have watched our students—men and women who came to seminary with more hands-on experience as leaders, both in and outside the church, than any of their professors—be sucked into thinking that nothing they had been or done or learned before the day they walked into that classroom meant anything. We have grieved for co-workers and friends in denominational offices who, overwhelmed by the red tape that, by accident or by design, ties up innovation and short-circuits experimentation, finally died trying—spiritually, if not literally—to be free.

We're not saying there is a grand conspiracy to make sure you keep doing things the way you've always done them. But we do believe there is something about the way the system has evolved that makes it behave the way it does. And too many of today's church leaders are trapped within that oppressive system. If that's true for you, you need to spend a day with Paul, munching on donut holes at the turtle races.

A second touch

Leading the faith community or faith-based organization you care about into the emerging future will require an entrepreneurial spirit. You will need eyes that have been trained to focus on what *is* for the sake of *what might be*. Instead of exhausting yourself and others trying to fill in the blank, you need to be able to see what you have for the sake of doing what matters. Like the blind man who needed Jesus to touch him twice before he could see clearly, you may need a second touch to help you to see things in a new way (Mark 8:22-25).

We've developed the PAWN Process to help. Also like the blind man, though, seeing things anew begins with admitting that something has been wrong with your sight. *I can see people walking, but they look like trees!* he told Jesus. *I can see something but I know it isn't right!*

What has been wrong with the way you've been seeing things in life, work and ministry? In a consumable culture, leaders see their context as something they have to respond and react to, control and/or manage. An organization theorist would put it this way: when you're using a consumable approach, you believe that "...the environment overpowers the organization by changing the conditions for survival and only those organizations that adapt will continue to receive resources."[52] When you see things this way, your job as a leader is to scan your environment for "strengths, weaknesses, opportunities, and threats."[53] In a consumables-driven structure your job is to make a plan that helps your organization survive based on the information you gather about what is happening around you. You develop programs, goods and services to meet the needs of your current and potential customers. If you don't, you know someone else will. And since resources in the environment are scarce (or so your fill-in-the-blank consumable mindset has led you to believe) you are usually scared enough to follow the plan. Or, in the case of many churches, you are frightened right into impotence and inaction.

There are countless problems with this way of seeing things. First of all, the theology of this approach couldn't be worse. The environment is not a threat. It is the locus of God's activity. It is the world God so loves! God is up to something out there. The biblical story shows us that, through the power of the Holy Spirit, God is on the loose in the world, at work in and through the people inside your organization; in and through people in your community.

One of our favourite Bible characters, for example, is King Cyrus of Persia. According to the Hebrew Scriptures, Cyrus came as an answer to prayer and rescued the Jewish people from domination by the Babylonian king Nebuchadnezzar. One of the first things Cyrus did was to send the Jewish exiles in Babylon back home to Jerusalem and give the people permission to rebuild their temple (Ezra 6:3-5). The Jewish people never forgot the role Cyrus played in their freedom. In fact, he is the only Gentile ever to be given the title "messiah" (i.e., "anointed one" Isaiah 45:1-6, 13). The people believed they could see God at work in and through this guy. The beautiful part of this story is that he never even knew it. God was at work in and through him, working miracles, and he didn't realize it. But the Jewish people of his time did. They could see God on the loose in the world. One of the most prescient theologians of the 20th century once wrote, "The history that we find recounted in the Bible starts simply in a garden and ends simply in a city. There was no altar in the garden, and eventually there will not be a temple in the city."[54] We need to be delivered, JC Hoekendijk said, from our fright for all that is "worldly." We need a second touch from Jesus to see the world the way God sees it, and to recognize God's activity within it.

Interestingly, organization theorists and researchers in the field of social innovation are discovering the same things the biblical story has been teaching all along. Many of them are now teaching that it's unhelpful to treat your environment like it is a threat to be managed. Your environment is, in fact, something you *co-create*. In other words, "there is no objective reality; the environment [you] experience does not exist 'out there.' It is co-created through [your] acts of observation, what [you] choose to notice and worry about."[55] This means that you can't prepare a strategic plan that responds to threats and opportunities in your context; you actually *create* your context through the things you see, plan and do. Many organizational consultants have stopped doing strategic planning at all! Instead, they are teaching people how to do *strategic thinking*. They are training leaders to pay attention to what is happening in their context and to learn from what they see. They are teaching people how to facilitate processes, develop relationships with people internally and in their community, nurture ongoing learning and growth, listen and converse (especially with those whose voices have been marginalized), work collaboratively and how to become "thoughtful actors and restless thinkers."[56] One theorist reflects, "These shifts in how we think about strategy and planning are important to notice. They expose the fact that for many years and many dollars, we have invested in planning processes derived from Newtonian beliefs. How many companies made significant gains and consistent progress because of elaborate and costly strategic plans? Very few." [57]

Some church leaders who have grown up using the strategic planning tools that characterize a consumable and mechanistic organization may be reluctant to put them down and try something new. Maybe, for now, those tools are actually working for you. But the future is renewable. Leaders of 21st century faith communities and faith-based organizations will be adept at "inventing as they go"[58] on the basis of what they observe and what they are learning. They will have their eyes open for what God is doing in them and in the people they meet *out there* in the world God so loves, and they will look for patterns that help them know which way to go next. They will learn to do a kind of dance; a letting go that happens when they sense that God is up to something, trusting that their job is to simply do the steps they've been shown to help them tap into and unleash the treasure of extraordinary power that dwells within them and the people they're out on the dance floor with.[59]

We believe this "emergence" or dance is part of the divine dance which God, through the Holy Spirit, is inviting us into. Those who lead renewable faith-based organizations and communities will know that the power and energy to get things done does not come from within themselves; it comes from God. And they will do everything they can to let that power flow through them, allowing it to take them in directions they never could have planned for on their own.

A new set of lenses

We have developed the PAWN Process to help you see everything (above all, to see God, yourself and your neighbour) with new eyes. PAWN can help you focus on what God is already up to in your environment and equip you to find and discover the opportunities that are right in your midst. This process might look mechanistic at first. If you look at the diagram on page 86, you'll see a two-dimensional rendering which includes three arrows pointing in and an arrow popping out of the top. It could look like just another tool for strategic planning but that's not what it is at all. The PAWN Process is a way of seeing that provides an ongoing way of seeing things anew. Unlike a tool that is applied to a certain situation or task ('the right tool for the right job'), the PAWN Process is something that is always 'turned on.' There is never a time to not pay attention to what is happening around you. The PAWN Process can help you learn how to dance.

PAWN uses three lenses to help you see the dynamic interplay of four key elements: Purpose, Assets, Wows and Needs. You don't have to be a Christian or a person of any faith to use the PAWN Process. It can help anyone, in any type of organization, get a sense of where the energy is, to find and discover the opportunities before them, to see in a renewable way and to avoid the fill-in-the-blank trap. But Christians will easily recognize the influence of the Great Commandment in the PAWN Process: "You shall love the Lord your God with all your heart, and with all your soul, and with all your mind…And you shall love your neighbor as yourself" (Matthew 22:36-40).

With these words, Jesus reminds us how much God values all people and calls us to do the same. PAWN helps you see, in a new way, the interplay between God, yourself and your neighbour. It focuses your eyes on:

- God's purpose for you.
  (**PURPOSE**)
- The gifts, assets and passions God has given to you and to the people in your context.
  (**ASSETS**)
- The miraculous things God is already doing in your midst.
  (**WOWS**)
- The things in your context that are breaking God's heart and that God wants to see changed.
  (**NEEDS**)

The PAWN Process reminds you to pay attention to what God is up to in you and in your context, and it helps watch for patterns. At the point where these four elements converge—purpose, assets, wows and needs—patterns begin to emerge. You are able to get a sense of where God is headed and what God is up to; and you can decide how best to join in. In other words, a vision for action emerges.

We often use this process to help congregations, judicatories and faith-based organizations develop a big-picture sense of direction or an "umbrella strategy."[60] But this process isn't meant to be used just once every few years during regrouping or revisioning periods. It is meant to help shape the way you see things every day in your life together. It is meant to help you answer the purposeful question that we've said ought to be on the lips of every Christian and every church leader every day, in every single situation: *What in the world is God up to…and how can we help?*

At this point, you may be asking, *why PAWN?* Well, we figure that it doesn't hurt to be reminded that our role is much like that of a pawn on a chess board. God is calling us to be on the front lines of God's mission to reconcile the whole creation and set people free. This is true for us together as the church. And it is true for each one of us as individuals.[61]

Here's what the PAWN Process
looks like, rendered two-dimensionally:

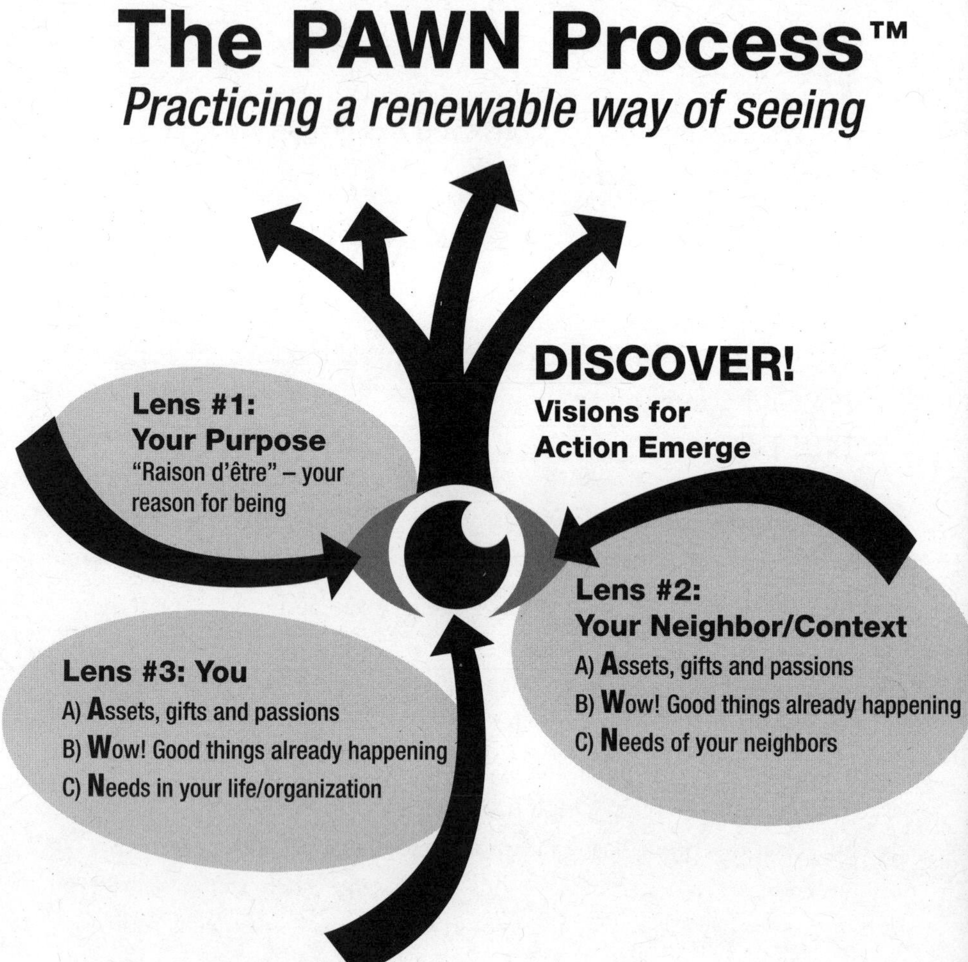

The PAWN Process™
Practicing a renewable way of seeing

Lens #1:
Your Purpose
"Raison d'être" – your
reason for being

DISCOVER!
Visions for
Action Emerge

Lens #2:
Your Neighbor/Context
A) **A**ssets, gifts and passions
B) **W**ow! Good things already happening
C) **N**eeds of your neighbors

Lens #3: You
A) **A**ssets, gifts and passions
B) **W**ow! Good things already happening
C) **N**eeds in your life/organization

God has a purpose for you

Seeing what you have begins with discerning the unique purpose God has
for the organization, community or movement you care about. You will notice
that the diagram above has three arrows pointing *in*. Each of these arrows

provides a point of view—a lens through which you can take a look at what you have. The first of these three arrows is for your purpose. Being clear about who you are and what really matters to you is essential if you intend to engage your context in a meaningful way, doing what

What really matters to us?

matters to God. "Without a clear sense of who they are, and what they are trying to accomplish, organizations get tossed and turned by shifts in their environment. No person or organization can be an effective co-creator with its environment without clarity about who it is intending to become."[62] As a faith community or faith-based organization, your purpose (who you are and your reason for being) is always defined within the framework of God's mission to reconcile the whole creation and set people free. Articulating God's purpose for you in this time and this place puts into focus the point of your life together.

Are you clear about the purpose of your faith community or organization? Are the people you serve with clear about it? Don't answer too quickly.

We know most congregations and faith-based organizations have a purpose statement somewhere. It might even show up occasionally on a worship program or a newsletter. But it's essentially meaningless. In most cases, it was written a long time ago by the pastor, executive director or a small committee. It doesn't inform a single decision that gets made. It isn't the metric used when evaluating a new program someone wants to experiment with or an old one that needs to be euthanized. And it isn't shared by anyone except (maybe) a small group of leaders.

Not sure if you have a clear purpose? Ask yourself these questions:

- Are the majority of people in your organization or faith community deeply passionate about your common purpose?

- Can you identify what sets you apart (really and truly) from other organizations or communities like yours?

- Do people in your organization or faith community understand their role in fulfilling your common purpose?

- Would the majority of people you serve beside be willing to change *any* practice or process for the sake of fulfilling your common purpose?

- Do people on the outside—in your community, neighbourhood or wider context—know what you stand for?

- Would your nearest neighbours (go ahead and make a mental picture of who they are) say you are fulfilling your purpose? If you're not sure, ask them.

- Here's a tough one: Would anyone in your neighbourhood or wider community notice or mind if you weren't there anymore?

If you can't answer yes to most of these questions—and in our experience most church leaders can't—it's time to get serious about a process that invites people to think with you about what God's purpose is for you. And this process ought to include everybody.

We have seen miracles happen in a room where 70 or 700 people have come together in a prayerful, playful process to wrestle with scripture and with each other around the purposeful questions: What is the point of our life together? Why are we here? What really matters to us? What is it that God wants to accomplish through us?

Seeing what you have for the sake of doing what matters begins with looking and listening, discerning and embracing the purpose God has for you.

God is at work in and through your neighbours

A second arrow in the PAWN Process diagram is the lens for you to view context; the neighbours God has given you to partner with, serve beside and care for. You will notice that your neighbours share a lot of similarities with you. You both have assets, gifts and passions. You both have needs. And in both places, God is up to something (i.e., WOWS). You might be aware that God is at work in and through you, but God is at work in and through your neighbour, too.

God is on the loose everywhere—both in the church and in the world!

This can be a hard concept for some people of faith to get their heads around. In fact, you may still be struggling with it. That will be especially true if you grew up "going to church" instead of "being the church." A lot of people did. They've got this idea that you go to church to meet God. And of course, you do. You hear God speak through the biblical story, the sermon, the songs, the words of encouragement and forgiveness that you share with each other, the invitation to come to the Lord's Table. But God cannot and will not be boxed in; not by our piety, not by our pious proclamations, not by any walls built by human hands.

The biblical story tells us that God shows up in all kinds of places and surprising ways. God showed up in Cyrus. But God also shows up in prison cells (Acts 12:1-19), in non-kosher kitchens (Acts 10), in the middle of roads that lead to nowhere (Acts 9:1-19). And in a move that was bound (and intended?) to annoy the religious leaders of his day, when the Messiah finally showed up, he didn't make his debut in the Temple; he didn't pitch his tent on a holy mountain; he pretty much avoided the holy city (Jerusalem) until he died. The gospel writer Matthew tells us that when Jesus started his ministry, he chose Capernaum, a city by the sea; the crossroads of the nations, land of Gentiles (Matthew 4:15). Imagine the shock of those who had been waiting for him to come for a thousand years, expecting to see him "at church."

Jesus has left the building!

This is God's world. God made it. God loves it (John 3:16). God is on a mission to reconcile the *whole* creation and set *all* people free. God is at work in and through your neighbours. In fact, God is speaking to you through your neighbours. If you want to see what God has given you, for the sake of doing what matters, you need to pay attention to what God is up to in the world outside your doors.

So, what *is* God doing out there?
Ask yourself these questions:

• What or whom has God placed in your context, neighbourhood, or wider community that can be a resource in your work?—These are the *Assets* you can tap into to fulfill the purpose God has given you.

- What is making God smile in your context, neighbourhood or wider community?–These are the *Wows*—the good things God is already doing, the places where you can jump in to help.

- What is breaking God's heart in your context, neighbourhood, wider community—These are the *Needs*—the opportunities God is giving you to make a difference, the places God wants you to go to work.

Seeing what you have includes paying attention to what God is up to beyond your walls and listening to what God has to say to you through your neighbours.

God is at work in and through you

The third arrow in our diagram is a lens for you to view your faith community or organization. There is only one key difference between you and your context: the church believes it knows a bit about what God is up to because of what God has done in Jesus and what God continues to call us to through the work of the Holy Spirit. In other words, the main difference between the church and the world is a clear sense of purpose. We know what the point of our life together is: God is at work in and through your faith community, calling you to participate in God's mission to reconcile creation and set people free. You will discern how, exactly, you can be most useful by paying attention to what God has given you to use.

> **What good things are already happening in your faith community?**

Unfortunately, many congregations, judicatories and faith-based organizations have fallen into the trap of scarcity thinking. Church leaders are scared to death of trying new things because they don't want to waste the few resources they (think they) have. They look around at bigger churches and more well-endowed organizations and they feel inadequate. They focus on what they don't have and what they can't do, instead of seeing what they have for the sake of doing what matters. This is a classic sign that they've been sucked into a consumable approach to ministry. They're not using up people and the planet like they're disposable, overwhelmed by scarcity. They're just doing *nothing*.

The PAWN Process can pull you out of this black hole by reminding you to look at everything God has given you for the sake of being a part of what God is already up to. God has given you a purpose. God has given you neighbours to serve and to partner with. And God is at work in and through the people in your faith community.

Having a hard time seeing it? Ask yourself these questions:

• What resources, gifts and passions has God given the people in your faith community?—These are the *Assets* God has given for you to work with. You don't need to fill in the blank with resources, gifts and passions you don't have. There are no more excuses to do nothing.

• What good things are already happening in your faith community?—These are the *Wows* where God is at work. In many cases, you don't need to start a single new ministry or program. Just build on the momentum that already exists!

• What needs do the people in your faith community have? God often speaks to you through your own needs, propelling you to move in new directions or try new things. Also, if people inside your faith community have these needs, probably other people in your neighbourhood have them, too. This could be God's way of showing you how you can be useful to both.

A vision for action

The church will need leaders in this emerging future who have an entrepreneurial spirit, who are able and willing to try new things, who are adaptable and resilient, and who dare to get things done. But these leaders will need help transforming the fill-in-the blank approach to life, work and ministry that characterizes a consumable church. The PAWN Process teaches you a renewable approach to life, work and ministry by helping you see what is happening in yourself and your environment in a new way.

Notice that the fourth arrow in the PAWN Process diagram—a *vision for action*—comes out from the centre. It is not a lens, but the vision(s) produced as the three lenses come into focus. As God's purpose for you converges with what God is already doing inside of your faith community and in the life of your neighbours, you can begin to see patterns that give you a clue about what direction God is headed and what God is up to. As you look closely at these patterns, ideas for action emerge. You can decide where to jump in, knowing that each of these actions is possible because they emerge from what God is already up to and the very real resources God has given to you.

Eventually, as you get used to looking at everything, every day through these three lenses, you won't need the arrows or this diagram anymore. The PAWN Process will become a natural part of the way you see things. *Trees will look like trees and people will look like people!* When that happens, you will know that you have learned how to let yourself really dance.

Looking for God

...through the biblical story:

Acts 17:16-34

If you're in a small group, read the passage out loud.

This is a story that illustrates how to do ministry in a new and uncertain context—which is the context a lot of us are facing these days.

1. What do you notice in this story? What jumps out at you? What do you hear God saying to you through this story?

2. Paul didn't have a fancy PAWN Process diagram, of course! But you can see how Paul used the three lenses in the PAWN Process naturally. Try backing out of the story to see how Paul's clear sense of Purpose, his own Assets, the Wows he discovered, and the Needs he saw all came together to give him a sense of what God was up to and how he could be helpful. Talk about where you see Purpose, Assets, Wows and Needs in this story. What can you learn from Paul?

...through each other:

1. What do you think about the idea that the church of *the 21st century will require no less of an entrepreneurial spirit from church leaders than the 1st century did*? The authors argue that entrepreneurialism (e.g. risk taking and investing in creative new ways of doing things) is, for the most part, discouraged within the institutional church and its various schools and agencies today. Do you agree or disagree? Is entrepreneurialism encouraged or discouraged in your own faith community or organization? What examples can you give to support your answer?

2. Do you think most people in your faith community or organization would agree or disagree with the idea that we are called—individually and together—to be "on the front lines" of God's mission? Why do you say that?

3. How would most people describe your common purpose? What would they say if you asked them what "the point" of your faith community or organization is? What do you think it is?

4. Do you need to do some work towards finding a common purpose that is connected to God's mission in the world? If so, what are you going to do? What difference would it make if you begin acting together more purposefully?

5. Which aspect of the PAWN Process do you find most exciting? Most challenging? Most important? Which aspect do you think your faith community or organization needs to really focus on? Why?

6. How do you think this process of seeing can help you avoid the trap of "fill-in-the-blank" thinking? Where can you start using the PAWN Process right now? Where can you start teaching your leaders to use it? Who would be open to learning more about this with you?

7. What do you think it means to say that the PAWN Process can teach you how to "dance"?

...through your neighbour:

1. Where "out there" do you see evidence that a shift from a consumable to a renewable approach has happened or is happening? Think of a place, outside of your faith community or organization, where people seem really engaged in their work—where they are passionate about what they do and do it with a deep sense of purpose—where they seem to know that they are respected, valued and making a difference. What can you learn from that place that will help you make the shift in your faith community or organization?

2. Traditional strategic planning considers "the world"—your neighbourhood, community, context, environment, etc.—as a threat to be managed and/or conquered for the sake of survival and growth. This approach has been dominant in business, non-profit and church life. In what way has that viewpoint seeped into the way your faith community or organization is functioning?

3. What would it look like if you could see your context with new eyes and begin to pay attention for what God is already doing out there? What would happen if you thought about people in your neighbourhood and community as potential partners and co-workers in God's mission? Who in your community is doing good work that you want to be a part of? Over the next two weeks, go talk to them; find out more; see how you can help.

The Back Story

[51] We learned this tidbit of information about the hiring policy at Whole Foods from Malone, p. 55. The rest of these real-life observations are our own.

[52] Hatch, p. 366.

[53] You may recognize the reference here to a SWOT analysis. SWOT (Strengths-Weaknesses-Opportunities-Threats) is a tool that is often used in corporate and church settings to help groups do strategic planning. We appreciate SWOT for the way it encourages a participative process; this is a helpful counter-balance to the command-and-control approach that characterizes a consumable organization. In fact, in the past, we have used SWOT analyses ourselves. We have come to see, however, that SWOT can and often does contribute to a fill-in-the-blank approach to getting things done. It has emerged from a consumable (i.e., modernist or Newtonian) perspective that views the environment as a threat, assumes a scarcity of resources and takes a mechanistic, rather than an organic view of organizational life. We can no longer justify its use theologically. It is also increasingly out of favour with organization theorists who believe the environment is not something to be controlled, but is, rather, something to be interacted with in a much more fluid way. In fact, social innovators would never use it, as they are working from an abundance mentality and eschew strategic plans for process strategies.

[54] JC Hoekendijk, *The Church Inside Out*, (Westminster Press, PA, 1964), p. 71.

[55] Wheatley, p. 37. Here she is reporting on the work of organization theorist Karl Weick.

[56] Westley, et al, p. 61. This is a phrase used by Francis Westley, et al to describe social innovators.

[57] Wheatley, p. 38.

[58] Westley, et al, p. 176.

[59] Westley, et al, p. 141. Westley, et al use the image of a dance to describe the way "emergence" happens in social innovation. Emergence is a term from complexity science that describes "things that are unpredictable, which seem to result from the interactions between elements, and are outside any one agent's control." (p. 128)

[60] Westley, et al, p. 141. "Umbrella strategy" is a term Mintzberg uses to describe the "broadly based goals" of an organization—these goals are supported not by a detailed list of goals and objectives but, rather, by process strategies—patterns for interaction that help cultivate the conditions for meaningful change.

[61] In fact, the book called *Reclaiming the "V" Word: Renewing Life at its Vocational Core* (Dave Daubert and Tana Kjos, Augsburg Fortress, Minneapolis, 2009) helps you learn to use the PAWN Process in your personal life.

[62] Wheatley, p. 39.

A New Way of Doing

"And as they went, they were made clean."—Luke 17:14b

Jesus has taught the principles of living and working together in a renewable way: *Be who you are and see what you have for the sake of doing what matters to God.* To be honest, there is a part of us that wants to say forget about doing what *matters*... just do *something*...do *anything!* We know how prone too many congregations, judicatory committees and organizational boards, can be to doing *nothing.* But doing *something* is not better than doing nothing if the something you're doing is pointless. In the emerging future, it will not be acceptable to squander the creativity, intelligence and passion of people by asking them to do things that are disconnected from your common purpose and what God is calling you to do together. People expect their work to be fruitful. And so does God.

There is, of course, the story of that first invitation to *be fruitful and multiply* (Genesis 1:28), which had less to do with bearing children than it did with being productive. *Make yourself useful!* God was saying. *Here are some animals; name them. Here is a garden; tend it. Here is a partner, help each other out. God expects you to be useful in reconciling creation and setting people free.* In fact, Jesus told his disciples, *if a point comes when you no longer feel like you're being useful, kick the dust off your shoes and move on.* (Matthew 10:14)

A lot of church folk are sick and tired of being part of a movement that never actually goes anywhere. But doing nothing is deeply ingrained in a lot of our congregations, judicatories and agencies. Have you ever read your organization's constitution for example? Like most legal documents, that one was written to prevent a worst-case scenario and to teach you how to deal with it if it ever happens. Some judicatory leaders say that their job orientation focused so much on the legal hot water they can get into now that they're in charge that they went home feeling scared to death to do or say anything.

Who wants to be a part of an organization that can't make anything important or new happen? Not these guys: more than half—60%—of the high profile

Christians one journalist interviewed over a five-year period (including one hundred CEOs and business executives, Hollywood types and sports stars, and two U.S. presidents) are not connected to a local congregation. Instead, they attend elite Bible study groups and give their money to select, very large, faith-based non-profit organizations. According to one researcher, these leaders just can't stand how most churches are run. James Unruh, who served as the chief executive of Unisys, used to be an elder in his Presbyterian church—not anymore. "It's very frustrating to be patient and to try not to run things because that's what you're doing all day in your business," he said. Others interviewed described local congregations as "unproductive" and "focused on the wrong things."[63]

We have a dear friend who joined the local congregation after moving to a new town when her children were small. When she asked how she could be helpful, she was told she could bring cookies to the next church function. This woman has a PhD in counselling; she was a professor at the local university. She has come to be known, in subsequent faith communities, as one of the wisest and most generous people in the room. But, maybe most importantly, she wasn't much of a cook. She baked the cookies, but they weren't very good, and she didn't last long in that congregation.

Don't let our talk about learning to dance fool you. This image illustrates the need for a *new* way to do things. But we are very serious about the importance of getting stuff done. And you should be, too, if you expect to lead your faith-based organization or group into the emerging future.

So, where's the plan?

Faith-based organizations and groups are not the only ones trying to figure out new ways to do what matters. Michael Lynton, chairman and CEO of Sony Pictures, for example, says he thinks the future is "anyone's guess." No one knows what the next new technology will bring. And so, he says, leaders in this industry need to be trying all kinds of things. They've tried putting movies on cell phones, teaming up with web-based companies like AOL and Netflix, etc. There virtually isn't anything they won't try and, he says, "At the end of the day, you see what works and whatever works you drill down and you do more of it. That's not to say it's a complete shotgun. I mean, there are a lot of things we say 'no' to; but by the same token it's not a rifle shot either because you don't actually know what's going to work. The trick is to make sure that when you see something that isn't working, you stop it; and when you see something that *is* working, you accelerate that." [64]

We got a good laugh out of this when we heard it: About a decade ago, when one member of our team was the pastor of a congregation in "redevelopment" (meaning that when she got there it was on the verge of closing and her job was to help restart it), one disgruntled member accused her of "just throwing stuff at the wall to see what sticks." "Yes!" she told him. "That's exactly what we're doing!" He wanted to see one of those hundred-page, professionally-bound, five-year plans. He wanted to set goals and objectives and stick to those, by golly, no matter what might try to knock them off course. But she had a hunch back then that 'sticking to the plan' instead of working a process to help you find out what sticks was a bad idea. Today, we're sure of it.

Odds are good that at some point over the past couple of decades somebody in your faith-based organization or group got scared looking at the graphs and charts showing downward trends and pulled out a workbook or a PowerPoint® presentation on how to produce a five-year or 10-year plan. You learned about measurable goals and objectives. You gathered a lot of quantifiable data and demographic information. You might have involved your members and maybe even people in your wider community. You spent months, maybe years, writing a plan that was supposed to focus your energy and resources, direct the actions of the staff and get everyone working together (and giving money) to help you get where you thought you were going. Then the world changed. Or some part of your world changed, anyway. And before you could say dust-collector, that's what your hard-won strategic plan became. Don't feel bad.

Jesus told the ten lepers who had come to him for help: *Go show yourself to the priest.* And as they went, they were healed (Luke 17:11-19). Again and again Jesus tries to tell us that doing what matters is a process, not a plan. *Come, follow me!* he said, promising excitement and adventure. But even Jesus didn't know the itinerary (Acts 1:6-8). *Are we there yet, Jesus?* his disciples whined. *No, not yet,* Jesus said, *and frankly I'm not sure when we will be.* But he trusted in God and urged them to trust God, too. *The Holy Spirit will be with you as you travel to the ends of the earth. Besides, every single thing you do—every step you take—will produce consequences you can't foresee.* When the Spirit did come, she brought tongues of fire, hurricane winds, the ability to speak in strange languages, an irresistible urge to use that ability to tell people about Jesus, a sudden and dramatic growth in the size of the community, opposition from the authorities, prison and death (Acts 2ff). Who could have predicted that?! If they had a plan (which they didn't), as soon as they did step one of it, step two would have become obsolete. The only 'plan' is to follow the Spirit wherever the Spirit seems to be leading.

It is perhaps not surprising that researchers and social innovators today are discovering the limitations of the *plan* and the power of *process*. And that's true not just in the way you *see* things (see the previous chapter), it's true in the way you *do* things, too. Increasingly, even the most cautious organizational consultants are recognizing the inherent dangers of the traditional strategic plan. By and large, these plans are written by the people in charge (who, understandably, want to maintain or enhance their power); consequently, these plans rarely challenge the status quo or move an organization forward in new directions. Anyway, people on the lower rungs of these organizations, who have little if anything to do with the plan, don't feel invested in implementing it and often work in quiet (and sometimes noisy) ways to sabotage it. But even those plans which are developed using participative processes quickly become meaningless and potentially counterproductive if they attempt to get too specific about what an organization should do and how it should get done. Jesus didn't have one. His disciples didn't need one. You don't either.

It's all about the process

You will be way more fruitful if, instead of spending time developing detailed plans, you figure out a way to get people on the ground working together to do what matters. The reality is that people who are closest to the ground know how to get things done way better than you, as the leader, ever could. Smart leaders are increasingly recognizing the truth of that. Some of them are using a method called positive deviance (or PD) to get things done in their organizations, especially in those places where the problems are seemingly impossible to solve. Positive deviance "helps the people closest to the problem discover their own ways of solving it." Instead of sending outsiders to tell the insiders what to do or making elaborate plans or giving orders from the top-down, PD coaches train people on the inside of an organization to unleash the energy—and the answers—that lie within the people. The first thing the PD method does is attempt to flatten the hierarchy—creating regular voluntary meetings, for example, where an equal exchange between people regardless of rank or position can happen. As a result, people at even the 'lowest' levels of the organization feel like they can contribute; usually, that is where the solutions to the most difficult problems lie. Using the PD method, hospitals have seen their MRSA (an antibiotic-resistant superbug sometimes called "staph" for short) infection rate drop dramatically; Vietnamese villages have seen the number of "well-nourished" children rise.[65] It isn't a plan that produces results like these; it is a process strategy.

A process strategy is a way of working together that gets things done. Unlike a plan, a process strategy assumes that things (maybe everything!) will change. And so it doesn't tell you what to do or how to do it; it doesn't give you a road map to follow. Instead, it teaches you to read the signs as you "grope and cope"[66] along the way, helping you navigate your way through an uncertain future. It teaches you a way of working together that frees you up to respond quickly to your environment, to take advantage of unexpected opportunities and to meet unforeseen challenges. Some researchers are arguing that the most effective strategies emerge only after or as people are already engaged in action. In other words, the strategies that really make a difference are the ones you discover as you go. That's how the process strategy we call the 4-D Cycle was developed; it emerged over the period of several decades as we worked in organizations of all types and sizes, with all kinds of people.

The process strategy we use actually looks a lot like *dagu*. *Dagu* is a word that comes from an Ethiopian tribe called the Afaris. It refers to information that goes beyond pure data, the ability to recognize emerging patterns (in weather, environment, health, political tensions, etc.) in that information, and the skill to interpret what it all means. Children in the tribe learn from their elders how to do this from the very beginning. They learn how to:

- **Practice deep listening and make astute observations;**

- **Make sense of the information they gather and to recognize patterns that emerge;**

- **Act on the basis of what they have seen;**

- **Observe what happens and learn from it in a way that informs future actions.**

The Afaris have survived all kinds of changes in their environment, natural disasters and human-made ones, for thousands of years because of *dagu*. Being nomads, they travel from place to place, looking for better conditions for their animals and their families. When they meet other members of the tribe along the way, they sit and share stories. They teach and learn from each other. They say "Afari is life." They know their lives depend on sharing it with each other.[67]

Researchers in the field of social innovation have discovered that change agents and social innovators have a kind of *dagu* that is almost instinctual. They don't count on plans to show them the way; they don't necessarily even have plans. But what they have is the ability to pay attention to what is happening, make sense of it, take action and learn from what they have done in a way that impacts what they do next and how they do it. We believe *dagu* can be taught using the 4-D Cycle.

The steps in the 4-D Cycle are:

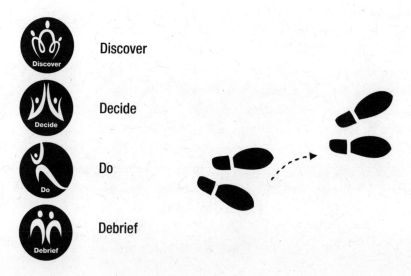

Discover

Decide

Do

Debrief

Again, it's very difficult in this two-dimensional format, to capture the dynamic nature of this cycle. But these steps are not linear; it's not like you're on the starting line of a foot race and when the bell sounds you start running, passing distance markers along the way, until you finally cross the finish line. *Ok! We discovered! We decided something! We did it! We debriefed it! Now we're DONE!*

It doesn't work that way. In fact, in the 4-D Cycle, there is no "first" step or "second" or "last." For example, we could put them in this order:

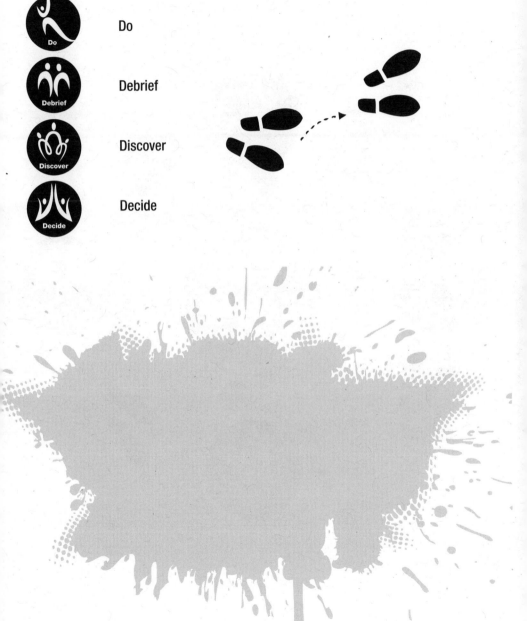

Do

Debrief

Discover

Decide

The point is, these four steps are not meant to be mechanically followed, one after another. It's not like the set of instructions you find in an IKEA® box to help you put together your new bookshelf. The steps in the 4-D Cycle are dynamic; they are, once again, more like dancing. In fact, if you diagrammed them on a dance floor, they would look something like this:

As you're learning a new dance, your steps may be clunky at first. But as you learn to do them, it all becomes more fluid. That's how using the 4-D Cycle starts to look and feel as you learn to use it. Think about every project you're working on, every missional direction you're moving in, everything you're doing, as a dance. As you follow the 4-D pattern on the floor, one step leads to the next so naturally as you move to the rhythm of the music, that it feels and looks like the steps aren't separate at all; they are all just one single motion. Also, you don't just take these four steps during the dance. You keep moving, taking countless steps throughout the dance, retracing the pattern on the floor again and again, adding flourishes and spins and fancy turns, until the music stops. It becomes impossible to tell which step is the "first" and which is the "last" because, as you're moving, it no longer matters. Obviously, these four steps cannot and do not describe the phases in the life cycle of a project. Instead, they show how you should work together as you're doing projects and moving in the directions God is sending you.

 **Discover**

In the last chapter, we described the PAWN Process, which is a way of seeing that can help you *Discover* what God is doing and how you can be helpful. This is one of the steps in the 4-D Cycle. It isn't necessarily the *first* step, although it might be. It is, instead, something that you do on an ongoing basis. When you *discover,* you are listening deeply. You are making careful observations, reflecting on *Purpose,* looking for *Assets, Wows and Needs.* You are engaged in Scripture, reading the biblical stories and talking together about *what God is doing in this story. What do I hear God saying to me in this story? What do I hear God calling us to do?* You are meeting and talking with your neighbours, spending time in your community, asking questions like *what is God already doing here? What is making God smile here? What is breaking God's heart?* You are listening to each other, sharing stories about what God is up to in your own lives and in your life together. You are trying to make sense of what you see, looking for patterns that emerge where all these things converge. You don't *discover* once and then move on; this is something you are doing always, at the same time as you are doing the other three "steps" in the 4-D Cycle.

There are, however, times in the life of your faith community or organization when you will want to stand still for a few minutes (or months) and get very intentional together about this particular step on the 4-D Cycle. Big transition moments can be a good time to do this (e.g. before or after your organization has a major staffing change, a relocation, a capital campaign, etc.) or as you are beginning the transformative journey from a consumable to a renewable way of working together.

During these standing still times, you'll want to use prayerful, radically participative, playful processes to help you listen together for what God is saying to you. You'll want to get as many people involved as you possibly can—we've worked with as many as two or three thousand people across a judicatory—and you'll dive into the biblical story together. You'll interview your neighbours. You'll gather stories about what God is already up to from people inside and outside of your organization. You'll work to articulate in a single, simple sentence, what you hear God calling you to do—God's *purpose* for you. And you will clarify, in a couple of bullet points, the directions you hear God calling you to move in. Real life examples we have heard faith-based organizations, congregations and judicatories articulate include:

- **Nurturing transformational leaders;**
- **Overcoming barriers to community;**
- **Addressing rural despair;**
- **Igniting spiritual renewal;**
- **Inspiring and equipping people to be a part of what God is up to every day.**

This standing still time is critical to faith communities and organizations that want to begin working in a renewable way together. It does two key things: It gives you an 'umbrella strategy' around which people can rally, and it will give them confidence that you're moving forward on this adventure together. And it introduces you to the principles, practices and process strategy of a Renewable Organization. But this is just the beginning. You will need to learn and practice how to *discover* at every step of the way.

 **Decide**

Another step on the 4-D Cycle is *Decide*. This is an important step because we have observed in many faith communities and organizations that once people stop trying to fill in the blank and begin making the shift to a renewable way of living and working together, they can easily become overwhelmed by how many things suddenly seem possible. All *kinds* of things look doable when you are focused on what God is already up to rather than on what you don't have or don't know how to do. And frankly, every single one of them is important and good. It becomes necessary, however, to learn how to sort through all of these possibilities and actually *decide* what you're going to do.

This dance step in the 4-D Cycle can be very tricky because, if you're using the seven Renewable Practices, you are using *participative processes*, which means that a lot of people—if not everybody—will feel like they have a voice in decisions about what you're going to do. The good news is, once you've made a decision, people will be enthusiastic about it and something might actually happen! But how do you manage the competing points of view?

When it is clear that there are diverse viewpoints in the room and people feel passionately about them, be thankful! Don't try to squash them; don't ignore them; do what you can to encourage them. The fact that you have people engaged enough in your common work to care about what you decide is a very good thing. Secondly, you need to nurture the relationships between people. Choosing a path forward can be challenging, even when everyone agrees (which they usually don't). Don't ask a bunch of people to make a decision together unless they know and trust each other.[68]

Remember, love is the most powerful force of all. It is love that gives people the ability to share their point of view, listen to other perspectives, and finally come together around a course of action. Nurture love. Third, help people learn to appreciate the value of experimentation. No one really knows the way into this emerging future. Tell them you need to just start throwing things at the wall to see what sticks. If something doesn't stick, no worries. God loves you even when you make a mess. You can just try something else. Next time it might be someone else's idea that makes the cut. Finally, as you are deciding what direction to go or what steps to take, don't be afraid to be irrational.[69] Yes, we said irrational.

When the level of uncertainty and ambiguity is low and everybody agrees about what to do and how to do it, go ahead if you must and use the rational method of decision making favoured by traditional economists. The rational method looks like this: 1) define the problem, 2) generate and evaluate alternatives, 3) select an alternative, 4) implement the alternative, 5) monitor results. But many strategic planners are beginning to admit that this model breaks down when the information you have to work with is incomplete or imperfect, when the problem is complex, when you have limited time and/ or human resources, and/or when you have differing viewpoints about which decision to make. And this happens a lot. Managers keep using the rational model because it gives people confidence in the decisions that get made, but that doesn't mean the decisions themselves are rational. In fact, researchers have proven that because some level of uncertainty and ambiguity is almost always at work, most decision-making processes are irrational; in other words, they are made on the basis of something other than facts.[70] So, if you're not going to make your decisions on the basis of facts alone, what will you use?

Well, some research has shown that an idea is much more likely to be implemented if it's an idea that people feel good about rather than an idea the facts support but people feel ambivalent about or are opposed to. These researchers would say that when making a decision, don't bother even looking at the alternatives that most people don't like. Furthermore, when you're debating between alternatives that various people do like, just look at the positive aspects; don't analyze them to death or you'll talk yourself out of doing anything. And whatever you do, don't ask things like *which of these alternatives is most likely to help us reach our goal*; instead, pick what you're going to do on the basis of where the most energy is—the thing people seem to feel best about. Once you decide what to do, go back and reformulate your goals accordingly.[71] The most important thing, if what you're really interested in is getting something done, is that the decision you make *feels* good to people; that they feel *called* to do it.[72]

Maybe this will help: Do you know how the early Christians decided to admit Gentiles into their fellowship? Remember—at first you had to be Jewish to get in; this was a hotly debated issue. Finally, there was a big meeting of Christian leaders in Jerusalem and they decided to allow Gentiles in. This event changed the whole history of the Christian faith. If it hadn't been for this decision, odds are you wouldn't be a Christian today. Did they make this decision on the basis of facts?—Not exactly. Some of their leaders had experienced what they thought was the Holy Spirit at work in the lives of these Gentiles (Acts 10-11). And in a letter to the rest of the Christian community, these leaders wrote, "…it seemed good to the Holy Spirit and to us…" to make this decision (Acts 15:28). *It seemed good because they sensed the Holy Spirit at work.* Enough said?

 Do

Look at all of the choices you have once you begin with what God is already up to instead of focusing on your own deficiencies. Then pick the one that feels Spirit-led. Pick the one that feels right because you sense God calling you to do it. Then, for goodness sakes, take action! A third step in the 4-D Cycle is *Do*. Doing isn't just about mindlessly putting your hand to the plow, though. It's about doing whatever you can, as you go, to make sure your action actually produces results. Now, if what you've decided to do is very simple, getting it done might be as easy as making sure you know exactly who is responsible for it, what the budget and timeline are, and then following up to make sure it happens, providing coaching and accountability check-ins along the way. In other words, you might be able to engineer it.

But most of the things God calls people to do are not simple. They are complex and sometimes seemingly impossible; and they cannot simply be engineered. Take *Go make disciples of all nations!* (Matthew 28:19), for example. Doing something like that is going to take a bit more imagination than filling out a task list before you leave tonight's church meeting. Once you decide to do something God is calling you to do, buckle up and get ready for a wild ride. The Holy Spirit is on the loose in the world, teaching, empowering, emboldening, comforting and nudging us along the way (John 14:26). *Doing* is about learning to pay attention to which way the Spirit is blowing, so you can go where the Spirit leads.

Interestingly, successful change agents and social innovators will tell you that, at some point in the process of working for change, they experience what is being called by researchers "flow." Flow happens when you feel like you're being swept along by a stream or caught up in forces that you may have triggered, but you know you don't control. One innovator has gone "so far as to say that unless the door seems to open effortlessly, you are not putting your energy in the right place."[73]

Flow isn't something you can create; it comes from outside of you. We would say this sounds an awful lot like the Holy Spirit. One of the reasons social innovators don't worry about writing plans is because you don't get things done by following a plan; you get things done because you have learned to go with the flow. If there is a lot of energy in the direction you're headed, keep moving in that direction. If you're meeting obstacles, like boulders in a river whose rapids you're trying to ride, don't try to go through them, predetermining what course you will take, go around them, letting the river lead you. Going with the flow—or following the Spirit—is about taking the path of least resistance and most energy.

You can't make flow happen anymore than you can tell the Spirit when to show up. But you can help cultivate the conditions for it. How? As soon as you've made a decision, do this: Start with sharing your plan with others. Pay attention to who gets excited about what you're doing and invite them to join in. Passion is the doorway to possibilities that become reality. Talk to people about what you're doing and why. Admit up front that you don't know exactly how you're going to do it so that other people have a chance to experiment and add their own energy, creativity and passion. Look for those moments when people really seem to own what you're doing and leverage their energy to keep moving forward. That's how you'll know it's the Holy Spirit at work. Forget your task list. Just go wherever the Spirit takes you. You will get more done. And you will do what matters to God.

 ## Debrief

A fourth (but not the "final") dance step in the 4-D Cycle is *Debrief*. Debriefing is about being accountable for how it's going. It's about answering questions like *What's going well? What isn't? What are we learning? What does this all mean for what you're going to do next?* and being brave enough to be really honest. We're talking about more than "single-loop" learning here, where you analyze the consequences of your behaviour at the most basic level (e.g. *hmm…we set the thermostat at 35 degrees Celsius and now it is REALLY hot in here!…we shouldn't do that again*). We're talking about "double-loop" learning; asking you to put everything on the table, to evaluate how things are going with a mind that is so open.

In this process you are able and willing to question even your most basic assumptions.[74] Double-loop learning looks, for example, like the elderly church leader who, at a worship committee meeting, dared to say, *maybe the reason our worship attendance is slipping so badly isn't because our neighbourhood is full of terrible people who don't love God. Maybe the problem is that our worship service hasn't been changed in the past 50 years and even we are bored with it!* This kind of deep debriefing isn't something you do just "at the end" of a job or a project (although you should do that); it is something you need to do all along the way. Being intentional about debriefing is the key to creating an organization that grows and learns, and only organizations that learn to learn will enter the emerging future.

It probably won't surprise you, at this point, to hear us say that the questions you ask as you debrief will look different in a renewable organization than they do in a consumable one. That's because the stuff you're measuring is different. In a consumable church you ask about whether or not you were able to fill in the blank and, if you did, whether or not you got what you wanted out of whatever was in that blank. You'd be counting heads and you'd be counting dollars. Do we have to point out what a total joy-kill that is? Even if the heads and dollars keep adding up, the pressure of keeping it up will eventually overwhelm you. And if the heads and dollars keep declining, it's even worse.

In a renewable approach, you need to ask questions that energize rather than stifle. You need a more creative and purposeful approach to evaluation. We like the idea of using developmental evaluations.[75] A developmental evaluation does not use traditional, narrowly focused, bottom-line oriented goals—and judge the success or failure of your work on the basis of how well you meet those goals. In fact, it assumes that when you begin your work you don't even know what your goals should be. Working in a renewable way, you won't know your desired outcomes until you actually engage your context and develop a shared vision. Developmental evaluation measures what you're learning and how you're growing and encourages you to put that new knowledge to use as you move forward. It takes the long view, because real innovation doesn't happen overnight. It asks probing questions, tracks results, provides feedback and helps you adapt.

So what metrics should you be using? What kinds of questions should you be asking? That depends. But generally speaking, you should be asking about things that matter to God.

Here are some examples of what you might measure using a developmental approach to evaluation:

- **Who is involved in our common work?**
- **Who has joined us and become more engaged in our work together?**
- **Who is missing? And why?**
- **What are we learning about the work we're doing together?**
- **What are we learning about ourselves? How have we been changed?**
- **What new assets, passions and resources have we tapped into?**
- **What new "WOWS" have we seen? What successes, changes and miracles have we seen happen as a result of our common work?**
- **What needs have we become aware of that we had not seen before?**
- **Are we being true to our purpose/directions?**
- **What's different because of the work we've been doing? How have lives been changed?**
- **What's emerging? How are we preparing for that?**
- **How are we sharing what we've learned?**

The truth is, no one knows what that future will hold. It might be helpful if you begin thinking about yourself as an explorer. Someone who does not go exploring assumes naively that "once they have a clear sharp picture in mind of where they are going, they can trust that picture through to the end. To be an explorer is to not know where, precisely and concretely, one is going."[76] You need to be bold enough to act on the basis of what you believe God is calling you to do. But you need to be humble enough to know that you don't know everything and you can't do everything perfectly. God is bigger than your biggest dreams and your very best plans. Build debriefing into every single thing you do, at every step along the way. Let what you learn inform your next discovery.

Until this "dance" comes naturally, you'll need to practice these steps in the 4-D Cycle very intentionally, although not necessarily in the order they've been presented here, and encourage your leaders to follow them carefully, too. This is especially true in the beginning of your shift from a consumable to a renewable way of living and working together. But the biggest challenge isn't in "adopting any one new method, but in learning generally to live in a process world. It's a completely new way of life. Life demands that [you] participate with things as they unfold, to expect to be surprised, to honour the mystery of it, and to see what emerges.[77] "It will be a challenge for most leaders today, including those in faith-based organizations and communities, to get used to working with a process instead of a plan. You'll have to if you hope to enter the emerging future.

Looking for God

...through the biblical story:

Matthew 6:25-34
If you are in a small group, read the passage out loud.

Jesus really wasn't much of an enthusiast when it came to planning. He was much more of a live in the moment, trust and follow the Spirit kind of guy. See for yourself when you read this passage from his Sermon on the Mount.

1. Who do you think Jesus was talking to when he originally preached this sermon? When you think about what life was like two thousand years ago, do you picture people who were busy-busy-busy, always striving for more-more-more, always planning for then-then-then? Probably not. But if they weren't, why would Jesus have to say these things to them? How do you think they heard these words? What do you hear God saying to you in these words?

2. Jesus basically says here that strategic planning is a waste of time. Seek first the kingdom means follow the Spirit—go with the flow! And he promises if we do that we will have "all these things." Why do you think we have such a hard time believing him? Why do you think we keep putting together our elaborate plans, worrying about tomorrow? Why can't we just go with the flow, trusting that God will lead us? What do you need to do in order to stop the madness—and trust the Lord? Who can help you do it?

...through each other:

1. Think about the last exciting, adventurous, faithful thing your faith community or organization did. What was it? Why did you do it? What happened as a result? How were people's lives changed? What is it that holds you back from acting like that *all* the time?

2. What do you think about the idea that "throwing stuff at the wall to see what sticks" may be more fruitful than following a carefully constructed plan? Why do you think that? What do you think about the idea that the best decision could be the "irrational" (i.e., Spirit-led) one?

3. What do you find most exciting about the 4-D Cycle? The most challenging? The most important? Which "step" does your faith community or organization have the most trouble with? Which do you think is most needed right now? Why do you say that?

4. Do you have an "umbrella strategy" for your faith community or organization? In other words, do you have a clear sense of purpose to rally people around? If so, what difference is that making for you? If not, what difference do you think that *could* make? What are you going to do about that?

5. Where is the energy in your faith community or organization? Who does the Spirit seem to be working in and through? Who is excited about moving in new directions? Where are surprising things happening? How can you leverage that energy to move forward? Who should you be inviting into this conversation? How can you cultivate flow and make space for the Holy Spirit to lead your way?

...through your neighbour:

1. What kinds of things has your faith community or organization been "measuring" to determine how successful your efforts are? If it boils down to counting heads and dollars, has that been helpful? Why or why not? What do you think your neighbours would say about that? What kinds of things *should* you be measuring?

2. The whole point of our lives (and the faith-based communities/ organizations we are a part of) is to be useful to God; to participate in God's mission to reconcile the whole creation and set people free. How much of what you *do* as a community or organization is really and truly for the sake of making a difference in the world? Seriously. Think about that.

The Back Story

63 This research and these quotes are from an article by D. Michael Lindsay, called "A Gated Community in the Evangelical World," USA Today, Feb. 11, 2008. http://blogs.usatoday.com/oped/2008/02/a-gated-communi.html#more

64 Entertainment Industry's Future Is Anyone's Guess, Morning Edition, National Public Radio, February 15, 2008.#e44.

65 Adrienne Day, "The Answer is on the Ground," *Stanford Social Innovation Review*, Fall 2009, p. 63ff.

66 Hatch, p. 118. This is language used by organization theorist Henry Mintzberg.

67 Westley, et al, p. 133.

68 Wheatley, p.150.

69 Hatch, pp. 280-281. Here the author builds on the work of organization theorist Nils Burnsson, whose work has been pivotal in advancing "action rationality." The point he makes is that what really matters isn't how good the decision is but what actually gets done. And effective implementation is more likely when the decision has been made because people FEEL positively about it than because all the FACTS support it.

70 Ibid, pp. 270-279. The author is building on the work of Herbert Simon, who is known for questioning the limits of the rational decision-making model; he labeled the problems these limits cause "bounded rationality." In other words, even though decision-makers want to live up to the ideal of the model, they just can't.

71 Ibid, p. 281. Organization theorist Nils Burnsson proposes these three "rules" as an alternative to the rational model: 1) Don't consider alternatives people don't like, 2) Only consider the possible positive (not the negative) consequences of each alternative, 3) Don't base your decision on your goals. Pick an alternative everyone likes and go back to reformulate your goals so that the decision you've made meets them.

72 Westley, et al, pp. 36-37. These researchers have found that change agents and social innovators—even those with no religious connections at all—inevitably describe their decision to take action as a "call"—"not a tentative invitation, but rather a violent yank over the threshold into an arena that was surprising, unpleasant, even frightening, but unavoidable."

73 Ibid, p. 128. The idea of "flow" plays a large role in the work being done by these researchers. Many of the ideas for cultivating the conditions for flow later in this section originated with them.

74 Ibid, p. 372. Here the authors are referencing the work of American psychologists Chris Argyris and Donald Schon, who coined the terms single-loop and double-loop learning. This is actually an approach that is being used by modernists in the field of organization theory; but we believe its tendency to deconstruct existing values and assumptions leans toward postmodernism and will be a helpful approach to learning for existing organizations as they move into the emerging future.

75 Ibid, pp. 83-85. The remarkable authors of this book warn "the traditional, narrowly focused, bottom line-oriented, goals-based model just doesn't work." They offer very direct advice to funders, who typically want to see more traditional, quantifiable outcomes (eg, "pay attention to the questions being asked, not just the outcomes promised," "set information targets, not just performance targets"). They believe funders have an important role to play in social innovation but the issue of evaluation—and tying grant money to strategic plans and quantifiable goals—is a huge obstacle to real change.

76 Ibid, p. 60.

77 Wheatley, p. 153.

Afterword:
Stranger Things Have Happened

Again and again the church of the 21st century will find itself in the same situation the apostle Peter was in during the 1st century, standing in the presence of strangers, confronted by questions he'd never thought about before, and being asked to go places he had never gone (Acts 10-11). Peter didn't have a lot of time to spend *discovering* what God was up to. When the Gentile named Cornelius asked Peter to baptize him, for example, which would mean breaking all the rules Peter had been following his whole life (and which Jesus had never given any specific directions about), the apostle had just a few moments to take in the situation and try to figure out what it all meant. Knowing that he might be wrong, but sensing that it was good to the people he was with and that he was being called by the Spirit, he made a bold *decision*. And he acted. He *did* something. He baptized Cornelius and his whole family on the spot. Then he went to Jerusalem to *debrief* what had happened with his friends and co-workers. The things they learned in that conversation informed everything else they did from that moment on.

Not unlike in the 1st century, the world around us is changing faster than anyone can keep up with. No institution, organization, business, school, agency, congregation or denomination is immune. We don't know what the future holds for you. No one does. But you can engage the present, learning to do life, work and ministry today in a way that is good for people as well as the planet. And you can learn to trust the process, following wherever God leads next, tuning your ears to God's voice so that you can hear what God is calling you to do as you make your way into the emerging future. Above all, you can trust God's promise that—although you may look like a clay jar—the Holy Spirit is at work in and through you, reconciling the whole creation and setting people free. Stranger things have happened.

Building on the work being done in complexity science, some social

innovation theorists believe that the key to meaningful positive change is what is called a "strange attractor." A strange attractor is that factor which cannot be easily predicted or even identified, but which scientists know is in the middle of a complex system, making all the difference. Think about whatever it is that makes it possible for a flock of birds to navigate complex migratory patterns, for example. Scientists can't exactly *see* the change agent at work, bringing order to what appears to be a chaotic and unpredictable migration, but they know it's there. This is how change works in complex social systems, too.[78]
For example, a little old lady who decides she is sick and tired of watching her neighbourhood go to hell uses her love of children and her gardening skills to start a community garden. She invites the kids next door to help, and without even knowing she's doing it, she inspires a whole block of people who have been watching her work, then a whole city of people who have been influenced by this new, vocal and persistent neighbourhood group, to take back their streets. She is a "strange attractor." She is a mustard seed.

She could be the people in your faith-based organization or community once they decide to leave behind the rusty 19th and 20th century models for getting things done so that they can just be who they are and see what they have for the sake of doing what matters. She could be you.

God is on a mission to reconcile the whole creation and set people free. And you are being called to participate in making that happen. *You.* Jesus' invitation to you is no more and no less than this:

- **Be who you are;**
- **See what you have;**
- **Do what matters.**

These three principles lie at the heart of a Renewable Organization System. This system will not bail you out of whatever trouble you might be in. It won't magically fix your problems. It certainly won't return you to former glory or propel you into the spotlight reserved these days for megachurches and rock star TV pastors. In fact, at least in the beginning, you may find yourself in more chaos than you were before you started inviting everybody to the table to work playfully and ask unsettlingly purposeful questions; before you started expecting and insisting that you actually do something, instead of just talking about doing something; before you dared to see the things in your neighbourhood and the world that are breaking God's heart. But if you want to be useful to God in this new future, you're going to have to make the shift from a consumable to a renewable way of living and working together. You're going to have to learn how to tap into that treasure of extraordinary power that dwells within you and the people you are working beside.

In previous chapters we have made a case—based on the biblical story and supported by some of the most interesting voices at work today in the fields of social innovation and organization theory—for the *shift* that needs to be made from a consumable to a renewable way of living and working together. We have described seven Renewable Practices that can help you bring out the best in the people you work with and serve beside. These practices can help you tap into and unleash the God-given treasure of extraordinary power, creativity, intelligence and passion that dwells within that clay jar of yours. They make it possible for you and the organization you care about to *be who you are for the sake of doing what matters.*

We also described the PAWN Process, which protects you from the fill-in-the-blank approach that characterizes a consumable organization and trains you, instead, to pay attention to what God is already up to so that you can jump on board. It sets you free from the paralysis that is so often caused by a scarcity mindset and helps you see your role as a co-creator of your environment, in order to spark innovation and ignite experimentation. This process can help you discern a big-picture sense of purpose and direction—or an "umbrella strategy" of broadly-based goals—to guide your work and focus your resources over a period of several seasons or even years. But the PAWN Process is actually meant to let God shape the way you *see what you have* every day, in every season of your life together.

And we have described a process strategy for a new way of doing things that we call the 4-D Cycle. This process is the antidote to those mechanistic strategic plans that characterize consumable organizations, suck the life and breath and creativity out of people, and end up collecting dust because they are obsolete the moment you take your first carefully planned and programmed step. This process strategy doesn't tell you what to do or how to do it. Instead, it describes a way for you to work together as you figure out how to *do what matters.*

This renewable approach to living and working together is a dramatic departure from the way things have "always" been done in the church, at least for most of the last couple of centuries. It will not be easy to make this shift. But it is not complicated. In fact, the whole Renewable Organization system is simple enough to draw on a napkin:

A Renewable System™

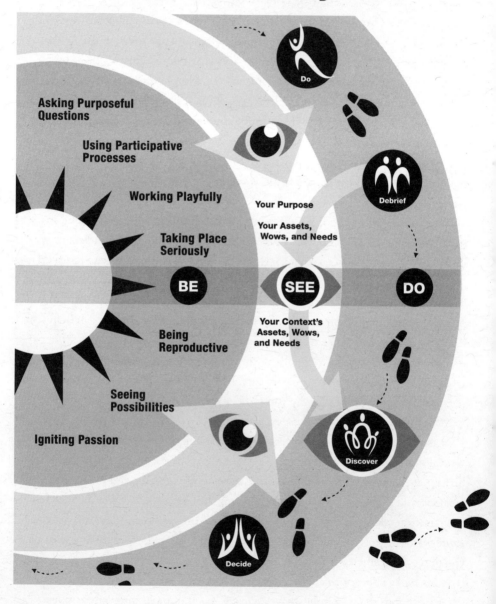

Asking Purposeful Questions

Using Participative Processes

Working Playfully

Taking Place Seriously

Your Purpose

Your Assets, Wows, and Needs

Being Reproductive

BE

SEE

DO

Your Context's Assets, Wows, and Needs

Seeing Possibilities

Igniting Passion

Do

Debrief

Discover

Decide

The future starts here. It starts now.

Looking for God

...through the biblical story:

John 4:27-42
If you are in a small group, read the passage out loud.

Talk about a "strange attractor." The woman Jesus met at the well was the strangest. Nobody would have pegged her as a person of influence or a potential change agent. The other women in her town didn't even want to be seen talking to her, which is why she was collecting water at the well at noon—the hottest time of the day. But there she is, recorded for all of human history as the woman who changed everything for a whole city.

1. Why do you think this woman was able to have so much influence? Why did people listen to her? What do you think compelled her even to try to influence the people back home? What is motivating you to do what you do? What motivated you to read this book? What is motivating you as you go forward?

2. As she went running back to the city, do you think this woman thought her words and actions would make a difference? Why or why not?

3. Do you ever wonder if *your* words and actions, and the efforts of your faith community or organization, have any chance of making a difference? How will you feel if you *never know* whether or not you have made a difference? And if you can't know, then how can you be sure that you are "doing what matters"?

1. What do you think about the idea that the key to real change in the world is a "strange attractor"—a mustard seed? Do you believe that even your smallest actions can make a huge difference in the world? Why or why not?

2. What excites you about the three principles of the Renewable Organization: *Be who you are. See what you have. Do what matters.* What challenges you? What difference do you think it would make in your faith community or organization to adopt them and use them in your life together?

3. Are you excited about making the shift from a consumable to a renewable approach in your faith community or organization? Why or why not? What do you need to do next? Who can help you do it?

...through your neighbour:

1. Have you ever met someone you suspected was a "strange attractor" like the little old lady who influenced her neighbours to take back their streets? Who in your neighbourhood or community has made a difference through words or actions that seemed, at first, almost insignificant?

2. How can you keep your eyes open in your everyday life to see what God is doing in and through the people you live, work, play, learn and serve with? If you could see God at work more often, what would that do for your own spiritual life? How would it change you?

The Back Story

[78] This is the research-based theory proposed in Westley, Zimmerman, Patton, *Getting to Maybe*, 2006. We believe it is supported by the biblical story and the evidence of our own lives.

Reading List/Bibliography

Brafman, Ori and Rod A. Beckstrom. *The Starfish and the Spider: The Unstoppable Power of Leaderless Organizations.* Penguin Group, 2006.

Gibbs, Eddie and Ryan K. Bolger. *Emerging Churches: Creating Christian Community in Postmodern Cultures.* Baker Academic, 2005.

Godin, Seth. *Tribes: We Need You To Lead Us.* Penguin Group, 2008.

Hatch, Mary Jo. *Organization Theory: Modern, Symbolic, and Postmodern Perspectives.* Oxford, 1997.

Hoekendijk, JC. *The Church Inside Out.* Westminster Press, PA, 1964.

Friedman, Thomas L. *The World is Flat: A Brief History of the Twentieth Century.* New York: Picador, 2007

Keifert, Patrick. *We Are Here Now: A New Missional Era.* Allelon Publishing, Eagle, Idaho, 2006.

MacLeod, Hugh. *Ignore Everybody (And 39 Other Keys To Creativity).* Portfolio-Penguin Group, 2009. p. 26-28.

Malone, Thomas. *The Future of Work: How the New Order of Business Will Shape Your Organization, Your Management Style, and Your Life.* Harvard Business Press, Boston, 2006.

Pink, Daniel. *A Whole New Mind.* Riverhead Books, NY, 2005, 2006.

Roxburgh, Alan J. and Fred Romanuk. *The Missional Leader: Equipping Your Church to Reach a Changing World.* Jossey-Bass, San Francisco, 2006.

Van Gelder, Craig. *The Ministry of the Missional Church: A Community Led by the Spirit.* Baker Books, Grand Rapids, 2007.

Westley, Frances, Brenda Zimmerman, and Michael Quinn Patton. *Getting To Maybe: How The World is Changed.* Random House Canada, 2006.

Wheatley, Margaret. *Leadership and the New Science.* Berrett-Koehler Publishers, Inc., 1999.

Whitney, Diana and Amanda Trosten-Bloom. *The Power of Appreciative Inquiry: A Practical Guide to Positive Change.* Berrett-Koehler Publishers, San Francisco, 2003.

Acknowledgements

One of the reasons there isn't a primary author listed on the books we are producing at A Renewal Enterprise, Inc., even though each one has had a primary scribe, is that it is impossible to tease out whose ideas are whose. Some of us on this team have been working together for over a decade, and each new member of the team brings a new perspective that continues to sharpen and shape our collective thinking. In every way, this book and others in the Renewable Organization for Faith-Based Groups series are collaborative efforts.

We have also been profoundly influenced by the work of Margaret Wheatley, Thomas Malone, Mary Jo Hatch, Francis Westley and the folks at the University of Waterloo Social Innovation Generation. We have done our best in this book to give them full credit wherever we are referencing their work in a direct (and even sometimes in an indirect) way. We apologize if there are references we should have made and didn't, and we accept all responsibility for anything in their work that we may, from their perspective, have gotten wrong.

We are thankful to the authors who have, at one time or another, been part of the Gospel and Our Culture network; their work has both influenced our understanding of what God is up to in the world and served as a helpful foil as we have moved in new theological directions. We believe that when the missiological conversation followed Lesslie Newbigin sixty years ago, after he and JC Hoekendijk came to that fork in the road, the church lost something very important that needs to be reclaimed; namely, a love for that which is "worldly." We hope this book will begin a lively conversation about these things.

We want to thank Kenneth Inskeep, Rob James and Amanda Sayers for reading this book in its first, sloppy draft and making suggestions that led to dramatic improvements in both content and form.

And finally, we need to thank the leaders of every single faith-based organization and community we have worked with over the years. Your willingness to invite us in to experiment, learn and grow with you has been a gift to us; it has helped us think better; it has made us better coaches, consultants and trainers; it has led to the Renewable Organization. Your gift to us has made it possible for us to give this gift to the church. May it help many, many people be who they are and see what they have for the sake of doing what matters to God.

Who Are We?

A Renewal Enterprise, Inc. (ARE) is a consulting group that helps people and the organizations they care about be who they are and see what they have for the sake of doing what matters.

The ARE team includes process facilitators, organizational designers, leadership trainers and coaches. They are the original architects of The Renewable Organization.

ARE works with organizations of all types and sizes across Canada and the United States but they have unique expertise and a special passion for working with faith-based groups.

For more information visit **www.arenewalenterprise.com.**